MY FATHER'S COMPASS:

LEADERSHIP LESSONS FOR AN IMMIGRANT SON

BRANDON—

ALWAYS CHERISH YOUR ANCESTORS'
JOURNEY FROM EUROPEAN
SHORES TO OUR AMERICAN
DREAM!

Perry J. Martini

ISBN-10: 0-9727323-4-9

ISBN-13: 978-0-9727323-4-5

Library of Congress Control Number: 2006934278

Book Design and Production: Andra Keller, Rocks-DeHart Public Relations

Academy Leadership books are available at special quantity discounts to use as premiums and sales promotions, or for use in corporate training programs. For more information, please call Academy Leadership at 866-783-0630, or write to: 10120 Valley Forge Circle, King of Prussia, PA 19406.

Dedicated to

Perry Enio Martini (1910 – 1994)

In memory of

Galvin John DePompei (1942 – 2006)

Contents

Foreword

When my father asked me to write the foreword for this book, I have to admit that I was hesitant and unsure of why he chose me. Although we have much in common when it comes to our personalities and to how we approach a project, we rarely see eye to eye concerning politics or world issues and have often debated our differences.

However, when I first opened *My Father's Compass*, I found myself not only enthralled with the story of my grandfather's life but also overcome with pride and respect for my father's work. This book is not about debatable politics or religion. It is about the power one seemingly ordinary individual had to inspire and serve others unselfishly. Furthermore, this book is about celebrating your roots and taking the time to remember and honor those in your family who came before you and, in part, helped shape the person you have become.

Since I was a little girl, I have heard the story of my immigrant grandfather's crossing to America. When my sister and I would travel to Ohio to visit our grandparents, "Grandpatini," as we fondly called him, would ask us to follow him out to his infamous tomato patch. As teenagers, this was torture for my sister and me, and we would flip a coin to decide who would have to go. The "lucky" one would reluctantly follow Grandpa-tini out the screen door, dragging her feet, knowing that he would soon be talking her ear off, talking excitedly in jumbled Italian and English.

I turn thirty years old this year. Looking back on those hot summer afternoons, I realize that they were a gift and I miss them deeply. My grandfather would point out each tomato and tell me stories about the rearing of each plant. Between moments of touching the vines, he would tell me stories of the "old country" and what it meant to him to be in America. Even though, half the time, I could not understand his words, I could see the passion, the pain, and the joy in his eyes when he spoke of his roots and of his own familial garden.

Although he may not have realized it at the time, Grandpa-tini was instilling in me a deep respect for family and for my own history. I take great pride in the fact that I am a woman and a wife; but, first and foremost, I take pride in the fact that I am a daughter. This root of my existence has formed every experience in some way. My family's lessons of love, hardship, and perseverance have provided a compass for me that has helped guide me through the murkiest waters of my life. Allowing me to understand their true colors, to listen to their stories, and to bear witness to the choices that have groomed their path in life has shown me the way in which I want to live my own.

As a filmmaker, I understand the importance of immortalizing memory, recording history, and capturing imagery so that future generations witness the imprint of our existence. Whether we commemorate these memories through dialogue, through print, or on the screen, we have a responsibility to those who come after us to tell the stories. We must push these narratives to the surface of our consciousness and wrestle with their meaning.

In *My Father's Compass*, my father has taken the time to delve into the Martini-Ferrara stories and to record a vital part of our family's history. Dad has grappled with the facts of Grandpa-tini's past and has paid homage to him. The "compass" that was passed on to my father by my grandfather has been central to Dad's journey seeking meaning in his life. And as I revel in the numerous stories of this book, I recognize that this "compass" has become central in mine.

Elle Raffaela Martini

May 21, 2006

Introduction

Nearly forty years ago I embarked on a journey to learn and write about my heritage when I started to gather information about my family. I considered myself very much the amateur genealogist as I structured the family tree based on the oral pass down of my paternal grandmother, Raffaela Ferrara Martini, along with assistance from my dad, Perry Enio Martini. The seeds had been planted early on to write about my immigrant past and to reflect on the foundation of my Italian roots. Completing this project provided me with a greater appreciation and understanding of the inherited leadership traits that would have a profound influence and impact on my personal and professional life.

My latest work, *Inspiring Leadership: Character and Ethics Matter*, was developed initially in the series of Academy Leadership books about leadership and followed *The Leader's Compass* and *The Corporate Compass*. I realized that the chapters on servant leadership, dignity and respect, and character were actually written about those leaders in my life who served to set the course for *my* leader's compass. When it came to interpersonal relationships and serving a purpose in life by a set of core values, no one had more influence on me than my father. His story as a young immigrant leaving his native land on a journey to find a better life is not unique in the annals of our American emigration history. Countless immigrants passed through Ellis Island between 1892 and 1934 from Europe, many of them from the hills of Italy who had experienced the hardships of life as peasant farmers courageously crossing the Atlantic Ocean in less than luxurious conditions to follow their dreams of freedom and prosperity. Fortunately, I was able to capture on paper my dad's vivid recollection of seeing the Statue of Liberty for the first time. I could have filled pages of personal and emotional recantations of the family's crossing but decided to keep those memories intact in my mind and soul and share with the reader the importance the experience had on Dad's life and those enduring values he passed down to me. This is the primary reason for my titling his story *My Father's Compass: Leadership Lessons for an Immigrant Son.*

My father indeed was stepping into the great unknown when he boarded the *Cristoforo Colombo* passenger boat in 1927. He was dutifully following the course set by his father Vincenzo's vision for America long before his mother and six siblings had begun their journey. These life-changing events were often spoken about at family gatherings during my childhood days and the primary focus was always about looking over the horizon and doing what's best for the family. Setting a course on a compass for one's journey is a classic metaphor in this story that projects a modicum of irony. My dad eventually served in World War Two and returned to the sea by joining the U.S. Navy. His youngest brother, Mario, also joined the Navy and became a blimp pilot, retiring as a Captain after twenty-four years of service. Eventually, I also joined the service and following graduation and commissioning from the U.S. Naval Academy, became a Navy pilot as well. As you read about the crossing, the turn of events that created our mariner connection will become most apparent in the story of my dad and his youngest brother, and eventually passed down to me.

This book is not just about my family heritage but also focuses on my dad's vision of a prosperous life and the courageous journey he embarked on as a young man. It would have been an injustice to not recognize that strong Italian-American family values and servant leadership provided the impetus for the energy necessary to complete the mission. I wrote this book with the deepest respect and admiration for my parents and grandparents who were never given the opportunity to become school educated. My dad, of course, educated himself and was never at a loss for understanding the world around him, for he listened intently behind a barber chair for nearly sixty years while becoming a voracious reader.

I often reflect and marvel at the wisdom of my paternal grandmother, Raffaela, who could not read or write in Italian or English. As a matter of fact, she spoke very little English, and when her signature was required, it was the proverbial "X." I know she is smiling down on me today as I affectionately recall her life with my grandfather and my dad. She lived for ninety-six years and experienced so much change in life. Raffaela Ferrara Martini remains one of the smartest and wisest people I have ever encountered.

I have great memories of growing up surrounded by these immigrants. If I am in the vicinity of Italian food, I can close my eyes and picture waking up Sunday mornings as a young boy to the wonderful fragrance of my surroundings. These memories and the enduring lessons my father passed down to me reveal who I am and what I have become.

My Father's Compass is a short story of faith, family, friends, and country and the enduring lessons of serving others above self.

Perry J. Martini
April 20, 2006

Chapter One

The Departure

THERE IS NOTHING LIKE A DREAM TO CREATE THE FUTURE.

- VICTOR HUGO

Raffaela stood at the passenger boarding area at the International Piers in Naples. She could hardly believe her own eyes as she stared at the huge ocean liner. It was indeed a welcome sight for her as well as the many Italians who impatiently stood in line to begin their immigration journey. Motionless and in awe of seeing something that had been merely a dream for nearly twenty years, she quickly returned her attention to her young children lingering nearby.

"Alberto," she called out to her oldest, "help me with these suitcases." "*Si, Mamma*, I have them."

A light rain began to fall. Raffaela was wondering what other obstacle would be placed in front of them. "Pericle (Perry), pick up Mario so he doesn't slip and fall." Perry had been charged with making sure he had Mario, youngest at five, in his sight at all times ever since they left their village of Rivisondoli.

Raffaela Martini and six of her children had now completed this first stage of their long journey to the New World. She turned around to make sure all was well with her clan and she couldn't help but see Mt. Vesuvius towering above her family in the background. It was an inescapable fact that this was the first and perhaps last time she would see this famous Naples landmark. It was but a passing thought and she quickly refocused on her motherly duties. Huddled together and anxiously waiting in the long line was her entire life these past six years—her children: Alberto, Perry, Elvedio, Eraldo, Almerinda, and little Mario.

As the rain started to subside, the sun magnificently reappeared, as if the famous volcano and the associated landscape was a painted picture behind their heads.

Her husband, Vincenzo, accompanied by oldest son, Giuseppe (Joseph), had left their small Abruzzo village of Rivisondoli over six years ago and made this same journey. It seemed like an eternity since she had been with her husband of twenty-four years. During the past few days, she had cried unabashedly with joy at the thought of seeing him again on the other side of the Atlantic Ocean and having her entire family back together again.

She looked remarkably young and vibrant at forty-four with radiant black hair and striking olive-skinned features, typical of

Italian women who spent their young adult days raising children and laboring in the field from sunrise to sunset. Men did not pass her on the piers without an admiring look and smile, but on the second glance they realized this was a woman—a mother—not to be approached in any way other than with dignity and respect.

With help from her older brother, Giuseppe (Joe) Ferrara, they made the 140 kilometer trip to the Naples piers on foot and by rail in three days. Her brother had already made the crossing and was wise to the ins and outs of the challenges immigrants had to face in making the long and exhausting voyage.

"Raffaela, please try not to carry all of the baggage yourself and let me help by tipping the strong young men on the piers," he pleaded. "They will keep your belongings safe until you make your way up the gangway and are safely in steerage."

Joe Ferrara was a square-jawed and rugged mountain man. Never one to shy away from a challenge, he was respected in Rivisondoli for his tenacity and pugnacious nature. Raffaela relied on his worldly knowledge and she depended on him for his advice and counsel now more than ever. Nearly all of Raffaela and Joe's siblings had made their way to the New World in search of a better life. Now it was her turn, and she once again turned her attention to getting the family onboard and finally settled as the ship neared the evening departure.

Fear came over her and she wasn't sure why. Perhaps it was the unknown that stirred her anxiety. She hardly noticed the beautiful sunset appearing beyond Capri as the Martini family finally made it to the top of the gangway. It had been twenty-four years since she married her hometown sweetheart, Vincenzo Martini, and they had talked about this vision of going to America during their short courtship. He was forever determined and she eventually, albeit somewhat begrudgingly, encouraged him in his quest in spite of the decades of obstacles that were constantly being placed in their path.

"*Padre Dio*," she whispered in prayer, "Please God our Father, be with us today and for the journey ahead on this mighty ocean."

She was forty-four years old and had never been outside her Abruzzo region, much less seen the Mediterranean Sea or Atlantic Ocean. Now she prepared to cross them both with family in tow, and prayer at this very moment seemed most appropriate.

Perry was now carrying young Mario as they climbed aboard. At sixteen, he was comfortable in his role as his little brother's guardian. The little Italian boy was very inquisitive and asked his older brother what seemed like a million questions from the moment he took his little hand and they walked together down the steep hill departing Rivisondoli.

"Perry, what is this big boat called?"

"Mario, be still for a moment. I'll explain later. Let's get settled first."

Perry had reached adulthood at a very early age. Much like his siblings, he attended grammar school in the local church, *Santa Niccola*, for about two years, learning the basic skills of reading and writing. When he turned nine, he started working as a shepherd with the older men, moving the local livestock from village to village from spring through fall. In the winter he shifted to the Rivisondoli cheese factory, stirring the creamy mixtures of the local recipe, which created the delicious *Scamorza* cheese known throughout Italy.

During his formative years, he had developed a knack for learning by closely observing people around him who served as role models. His mom and dad were shining examples of how to raise a family in the ebb and flow of the peasant lifestyle. He hung onto every word spoken by his field bosses while he shepherded by day and camped by night. In the cheese factory, the men spoke incessantly of this far away, distant land called *"Medica."* He was curious as to their interest of such a place, insatiable in gathering information, and never running out of questions.

He stood at the top of the gangway, Mario now wrapping his arms around the back of his neck getting ready to take a nap.

The crowd surged behind him to get onboard quickly before the ocean liner pulled its lines and got underway. There was a lot of commotion. He was told to wait once again as their patience was tested in the chaos of hurrying up and then waiting.

Although forced to wait for long periods of time, he held Mario effortlessly. He was a typical Italian man who had experienced the sweat and toil of physical labor that profiled his young life. His jet black hair was combed straight back and was complimented by his ruddy complexion. His deep-set eyes and handsome stature produced the impression that this was someone who belonged on stage.

Perry looked down at his boarding pass and noticed the date imprinted under the ship's name—March 10, 1927.

Habitually, he reflected deeply about the circumstances surrounding the previous few days. He greatly admired the wisdom and strength of his mother and how she had courageously fulfilled the wishes of her husband in their quest for a new life. Raffaela had boldly sold all their worldly possessions, including their livestock, and traversed the mountains and valleys to Naples on foot and eventually by rail. His favorite uncle, Joe Ferrara, accompanied her and was determined to get his sister, as well as his nephews and niece, safely onto their ship in Naples and on to America. Perry now reflected on what he had observed during their departure when they walked down the hill from their Rivisondoli home, as his mother turned attentively to her two oldest boys.

"You two must keep your eyes on your younger brothers and sister for we have quite a journey ahead of us. Alberto, stay near Almerinda, and, Perry, hold young Mario's hand. You two are in charge and stay close to them until we get to America!"

Perry remembered grabbing hold of Mario's hand. Mario was a little guy and a few months short of his sixth birthday. "Mario," Perry spoke abruptly, "do not leave my side because mamma just made me your boss. I'll make sure you have a fun trip and please stop whining." Mario was understandably confused. Where exactly were they going and why was mom shutting down their house? Perry recalled how quickly Mario changed his mood when he picked him up for he was already tired of walking.

Perry's train of thought was broken by the sound of a deep and loud male voice.

"*Avanti!*" "Move ahead!" The thundering voice seemed to be using a strange looking cardboard funnel. They were directed to move to the rails near the ladders leading downward and to have their boarding passes handy for the officials to see. He held his and Mario's passes tightly as they were once again herded forward, with Raffaela in the lead and Alberto and the other children behind him. As they all stood again in another line awaiting the climb down to steerage, he stood at the rail letting Mario gently down to be next to him, and they both waved at their uncle standing quietly on the pier.

Joe Ferrara, arms folded, remained hauntingly still while keeping his steady eyes on all of them. Perry's mind began to wander again. He remembered how much his uncle had helped his mom and family upon arrival at the train station in Naples by getting them into a horse-drawn carriage to take them to the piers at Naples Bay. He thought of the previous few frantic minutes that seemed like hours and how his uncle was pacing back and forth at the pier, tipping porters alongside the large passenger liner they were about to board, at the same time assisting the loading dock personnel with the Martini clan's belongings. Again, Perry was startled by someone yelling at them.

"Be sure you are on the right side of the ship as you leave the harbor!"

Perry recognized the voice and couldn't help once again to expect the unexpected from his Uncle Joe. How befitting that they boarded the *Cristoforo Colombo* passenger ship for passage to the New World. Perry had heard of this man, Colombo, and he decided to save the story for his little brother during the crossing.

Hurriedly, he took charge along with his older brother Alberto and herded the family down into steerage for preparation for the long two-week-plus voyage. He told everyone to drop their personal items near their suitcases in steerage where the porters had placed them and to return quickly to the top deck on the right side of the ship. While he was climbing the narrow ladder, the vessel surged forward accompanied by a single loud blast on the ship's horn.

Once settled on the main deck, Perry scanned the horizon and watched with a bit of anxiety as the hills of Naples began to disappear on the horizon. He was leaving his native country to fulfill the lifelong dream that had become part of the family's everyday conversation. He reflected on how he had spent his early years helping his mom raise the family while his dad prepared the way to a new life in America. He had good memories of attending the primary school located in the only Catholic church in the village. He started at the age of seven and completed his education two short years later. He remembered his dad telling him he needed to start becoming a man and to go to work. There was no time to sit outside and look at the valley below their house with his younger brothers and watch the world go by. At nine, Perry had become a young man among men and shepherded sheep and goats while tending to the fields nearby. In the winter months, he would work tirelessly in the local cheese factory, attending to odd jobs to help the family with food and essentials. It was a stark and simple life, filled with hope and anticipation of one day enjoying the great promise of America, for they talked incessantly about it, especially in the 1920s when father would write occasionally from "the States."

Now, as Perry sat perched atop an ocean liner, his family's dream was finally becoming a reality. As he watched Naples start to disappear and the surrounding islands of Capri and Ischia come into view, he recalled the wonderful experience of eating in a restaurant for the first time the night before their departure. Along with his mother and five brothers and sister, they enjoyed dining at a large table, with dinner plates, silver, and even bottles of local wine. He reflected on the fascination he experienced in using a "small tablecloth" that appeared to be a napkin. Copying an older man sitting nearby, he placed this "real napkin" in his collared shirt and used it as a bib to ensure the spaghetti sauce wouldn't stain his only clean dress shirt. After dinner they were treated to gelato and, for the first time in their lives, enjoyed the Italian ice cream they had only heard about in the country.

As he sat above the decks of the *Cristoforo Colombo*, Perry scanned the horizon to the West. The ocean liner started to accelerate and he could smell for the first time in his life, the salt spray that was now emanating from Naples Bay as they sped toward the open seas. As the sun began to set, he ruminated about the life ahead of him and it left him in a state of bewilderment. He looked down at young Mario, who was still at his side, and whimsically said, "Is America really the land of plenty? What kind of work is in store for me?" Mario didn't respond for he was far too busy looking at the other ships in the harbor. Perry continued to speculate silently. *Would the values he learned to love as a young boy growing up in the hills of Italy be forever changed? Was his father's vision colored by adventure or was the future as bright as his father hoped it would be? What would become of them?*

Suddenly, he turned to look over the railing on the right side of the boat as someone was shouting his name. "Perry! Look over here! *Buono fortuno e buono voyaggio!*" There, on the right side, was his Uncle Joe, riding atop a small speedboat with one of the locals, whom he had apparently tipped to drive him out to the *Cristoforo Columbo*. Perched like a sail at the tip of the small boat, Uncle Joe's figure quickly started to disappear almost as quickly as he had emerged. Strangely, Perry thought he heard him say, "See you soon!"

"*Zio Giuseppe, molte grazie per tutto! Arrivederci e l'amiamo!*" "Uncle Joe, many thanks for everything! So long and we love you!" His uncle was now turning back towards Naples and waving frantically as the passenger ship, *Colombo*, picked up speed entering the Tiranean Sea and headed into the sunset toward the Mediterranean.

The ship's compass was heading west and Perry was desperately searching his soul for his own compass bearing. The trip was long and he spent restless nights gathering the courage to face whatever challenges and opportunities faced him.

LESSONS OF LIFE

1. Live your dreams.
2. Love your family foremost.
3. Know your roots.
4. Observe and learn.

Chapter Two

A Father's Crossing

There is a volume of recorded history regarding the origin of the country of Italy. From its formation in 753 B.C. until its collapse in 476 A.D., the Roman Empire encompassed a vast region of territory and controlled the lives of millions of people. Within this empire, there was a region in east-central Italy, with an area of 4,200 square miles, called Abruzzo.

Abruzzo is made up of two distinct areas of almost equal size. The central Apennines, with high valleys and rich basins, form the western area, bordered by the province called L'Aquila. Generally, this province has been highly susceptible to very cold winters and frequent earthquakes for the past 2,000 years. Agriculture is the dominant way of life in L'Aquila where there are beautiful green meadows covered by flocks of grazing sheep.

In L'Aquila province there were many small villages that began to form in the 15th and 16th centuries. Although the Abruzzo population called themselves "Italian," the Normans continued to govern the territory and so it remained under foreign rule. The Bourbons were the last of these rulers. At the beginning of the 18th century, the people of these small villages were active in liberalizing how they lived. They formed the nucleus of what was to eventually become an organized form of self-government in the countryside. This story focuses on a small number of these "Italians" nestled in a very small mountain village called Rivisondoli.

Rivisondoli consisted of about fifty families in 1790. Approximately three hundred people lived in this friendly town. There were six families that occupied small huts on the side of the Apennines that comprised the Massari, Falcione, Romito, Daltorio, Ferrara, and Martini bloodlines. In 1903, two descendants of these families, Raffaela Ferrara and Vincenzo Martini, were married in a happy ceremony that typified the native wedding feasts that frequently occurred among the young.

The diminutive Vincenzo Martini was a unique and inquisitive man. His mother died giving birth to him and his distraught father abandoned him before he was barely six months old. It was an act of family destiny that his paternal grandmother, Maria Massari Martini, raised him. As a young boy, he became the typical peasant farmer as a shepherd, working long hours in the summer months and wintering over in the local cheese factory. He was full of energy and ambition, while his dark features, quick-stepped gait, and long handlebar mustache became his trademarks.

In 1899, at the age of 20, Vincenzo first learned of a place far away that captivated his curious nature. His good friend, Nicolo Daltorio, approached him one day in the local cheese factory.

"Vincenzo, I heard from a few others that you have been thinking about an adventure to America. I made the trip a few years ago and am planning to go again. Why don't you come with me and see for yourself?" He was startled for until this moment it all seemed like a dream to make such a trip.

He replied, "Nico, I would love to go but I don't think I can afford passage. Once we got there, how would I manage? Where would I stay? I don't know; it sounds too fantastic to even fulfill such a wish!"

"We need to talk more about this, Vincenzo. I am going to stay with cousins in a place called Pittsburgh in the region of Pennsylvania. I'm sure he'll let you stay with us, and you can see this amazing place for yourself. I intend to investigate the possibility of living in America if I can convince Rosaria Ferrara to marry me and join me. Then I will leave this village for good."

The more Vincenzo inquired about this mystical land, the more interested he became. He started to visualize the adventures from the stories that many of his contemporaries like Nicolo were sharing with him. It became clear to him that his fellow peasants were leaving their native country to seek out new opportunities in the New World of America. He listened intently and learned of the mighty United States of America that took care of its people in a caring and democratic way. It gave him great hope to know that there was actually a better place to live. Many of Nicolo's friends in the cheese factory had returned to report their vision of the famous Statue of Liberty, the hustle and bustle of a city called New York, and the many job opportunities in the coalmines and railroads in states called Pennsylvania and Ohio.

Impulsively, and with encouragement from Nicolo, Vincenzo made his first trip to America in 1901. Once arriving in Ellis Island with a mere fifteen U.S. dollars in his pocket, he walked with Nicolo to the nearest railroad station and traversed by train to western Pennsylvania in hopes of finding work in the Penn Railroad Company. Bunking in a place near Pittsburgh called New Kensington, his short stay in this new place was a success. He made roughly $1.00 per day as an errand and water boy, and when he had collected enough for passage, he returned to his native Italy in 1901.

Overcome by the power of his experience, Vincenzo spoke incessantly about America. Shortly after marrying his sweetheart, Raffaela Ferrara, he shared his vision with her that perhaps someday they would have a family in America.

"Raffaela, my trip two years ago to America is something that is hard for me to put into words. I believe we could have a better life surrounded by opportunities for you and me and our future children. I know you think I'm crazy, but I need you to think about it and make the next trip with me."

She had her doubts and placed these futuristic thoughts in her heart as the thoughts and talk of a dreamer, for she could not comprehend ever leaving her family and native village. However, she did ponder the idea frequently and contemplated the possibility, especially when her older brother, Emilio, and younger sister, Rosaria, who had married Vincenzo's best friend, Nicolo, departed for America later in 1903.

In 1905, Raffaela and Vincenzo started their own family in Rivisondoli. Subsequently, over the next fifteen years, she would give birth to six sons and one daughter. Their third oldest son, Pericle (Perry) Enio Martini, was born on October 16, 1910.

This story focuses on Perry, my father, and the shared vision of his father, Vincenzo: to become an American.

Vincenzo Martini eventually made four successful trips to America in the decade following his maiden voyage in 1901. In

1916, his dream of taking the family with him was stymied by the draft notice he received from the Italian Army. The world was at war, and he was called to fight the Austrians and Germans on the Northern Front. As the war in Europe raged, Vincenzo was entrenched on the Austrian border north of Venice along the Tagliamento and Isonzo Rivers. Coincidentally, a little-known American Red Cross volunteer ambulance driver often referred to as "*Ernesto*" was working in a hospital near these rivers at Fossalta. Later, Ernest Hemingway would write of the great Battle of Caporetto and the breakthrough of the Austrian Army through the Italian Front. This was to be the setting for his *Farewell to Arms*. It was here at the Battle of Caporetto in October of 1917 that Italy lost nearly 300,000 men—30,000 dead, 50,000 wounded, and 270,000 captured.

During this brutal battle, Vincenzo Martini laid silently among the mortally wounded who were cut down by machine gun fire near the front. Vincenzo was saved by his helmet; the bullet ricocheted and entered his neck through his collarbone and passed through his lungs. Ironically, he befriended the young "*Ernesto*" Hemingway while recovering in a makeshift battlefield hospital.

"Ernesto," Vincenzo spoke in broken English, catching Hemingway's attention.

"I have been listening to you speak Italian and you mix a few English words with your Italian. I have been to the States and I can try and speak to you in English and teach you some Italian as well."

The future author was duly impressed that Vincenzo knew so much about his native America and could even speak his language.

"I would be a happy man, if you could teach me. What is your name and where are you from in Italy?"

"I am Vincenzo Martini and I am from a small village in Abruzzo called Rivisondoli," he proudly proclaimed.

Hemingway quickly replied, making his way to the bedside of the fallen solider, "Good Vincenzo, teach me how to speak more clearly in your native language and tell me more about your trips to America."

This short friendship undoubtedly sparked future writings as Hemingway often reflected upon venturesome dreamers he came in contact with during his younger days.

Meanwhile, news of husband and father Vincenzo's possible capture or death spread through the small village in Rivisondoli. Rumors were common in the small villages of Italy since communication from the front lines was scarce and official news took weeks to get to its intended destination.

Young Perry, now seven, ran to the post office to retrieve the much-anticipated telegram that included the details of his father's battle wounds and the welcome news that he was indeed recovering in a hospital in Brescia, Italy. His mother, Raffaela, had instructed him to ask someone to read it to him since no one was at home who could read. In his excitement, he stopped an elderly gentleman outside the post office and asked, "Please, *signore*, read this telegram to me. *Fa subbito*, quickly, for we are anxious to know of Papa's fate!" The old man read the telegram aloud and young Perry ran like the wind to spread the good news.

"Mamma, Papa is alive!" he proclaimed as he burst into their tiny home. Tears of joy with the good news greeted older brothers Giuseppe and Alberto when they returned from the fields later that day. They were twelve and nine years old, respectively, and attending to the chores of the household since Papa had departed for war.

Perry cried after blurting out the good news. It was October 16th and he couldn't imagine a better birthday present!

Vincenzo returned home in November of 1917 to recover from his wounds, and nearly a year later, the church bells tolled throughout Italy signaling the end of the war in 1918 and the peace treaties were signed. Ironically, it was the land afar called America that finally entered the conflict and brought it to a peaceful and speedy conclusion. Vincenzo's ambitious dream to journey to this America had been placed on hold due to the war, but he now renewed his desire to make the trip with passion and vigor.

Accumulating the necessary means with hard work and savings in the next few years, Vincenzo and his oldest son, fifteen-year-old Giuseppe (Joe), departed Italy in hopes of fulfilling their vision to establish residency in the United States for their large family. Their plan was to work and to save enough money for the family to reunite in America within a year. So, in November 1920, they departed for Naples and embarked on the passage to New York.

Their journey was not a smooth one, for not only did they miss their boat in Naples, but the vessel that they finally boarded made an unexpected and long layover in Marseilles, France. To make matters worse, Vincenzo was stricken with the flu and had to be carried back to the ship following a long stopover; he was nearly deported back to Italy due to poor health.

"Giuseppe, please go without me for I am too ill to travel!"

"Nothing doing, Papa," the oldest son exclaimed. "We will wait and catch the next boat and go together as planned. I will not leave you here in France!"

So, in spite of this diversion, the passage to America was finally brought to fruition and father and son settled in a small town in Northeastern Ohio called Warren. They took on many odd jobs at the new steel mill plants as well as janitorial duties in the local hotels and restaurants. They quickly learned from fellow Italian immigrants that learning the language and customs of America was the shortest route to assimilating into the culture. Together they began their quest in earnest on becoming Americans.

The goal of working and saving was underestimated as it took years to earn enough money to buy a home large enough for the Martini family. Furthermore, a fascist tyrant by the name of Benito Mussolini was wreaking havoc on the peace that had been inherited at the end of the Great War. For many Italians, normal immigration escape routes were being blocked, and Raffaela Martini and her children were having a difficult time receiving approval for an eventual passage to America. Immigration laws quickly changed in the 1920s and the States were now accepting only 8,000 Italians per year rather than the 25,000 per year they were accepting at the turn of the century. As a last resort, Vincenzo decided to patiently work through the five-year waiting period and applied for U.S. citizenship in 1926. Proudly, he became an American citizen and lifted any barriers Italy might have attempted to place in front of the Martini family that would prevent their completing their immigration plan.

LESSONS OF LIFE

1. Live your vision.

2. Persevere in all things.

3. Patience is a virtue.

4. Love of country is the highest calling of civilized man.

Chapter Three

My Father's Crossing

OH, HEAR US WHEN WE CALL TO THEE, FOR THOSE IN PERIL
ON THE SEA.

- NAVY HYMN

My father arrived in New York Harbor to find it basking in the morning sunrise on March 29, 1927.

The crossing was uneventful but nevertheless arduous. The family had found the herded masses of immigrants in steerage stifling. Perry couldn't get used to the overwhelming stench that constantly permeated the living quarters on the bottom decks. It was not what he had expected and he was fearful of being sick for the entire voyage. He had remembered his father telling him that "you don't get seasick if you eat lots of chocolate, cheese, and bread, and, above all, stay outside in the fresh air when the boat starts to rock and roll." Following this advice, he took his youngest brother, Mario, with him topside often to breathe in the fresh air while rationing huge chunks of chocolate and cheese they brought aboard washed down with steerage bread and water.

Perry looked down at his youngest brother on their first morning at sea. "Mario, stick with me and you won't get seasick. Take your time eating the chocolate for it has to last us until we get to the other side of this big ocean."

They would often return below decks together for meals in steerage to wait out the night with the rest of the family and were never quite sure when they would finally arrive in "*Medica!*" Perry, with Mario in tow, settled into a routine while crossing the great Atlantic. Rise and shine early each morning, eat a hearty breakfast with mother, and then quickly go topside to breathe in the fresh air.

Steerage on an ocean-going passenger liner that was built in 1915 was vastly different from riding first class on a large cruise ship. The *Cristoforo Colombo* was hardly a luxury liner. Small in stature and only a fourth of the size compared to such passenger liners as the ill-fated *Titanic*, there was little room in the bottom decks where 2,000 of its poorer passengers made their home for the long journey. Truthfully, it was crowded and more like a large room with bunk beds spaced everywhere and a general dining area in the middle. It was the cheapest way to traverse the great oceans in the early part of the 20th century. Privacy was limited. Families huddled together in bunk bed conclaves and everyone used the common wash areas to stay clean. There was little change of clothing for their baggage carried few extra clothes.

The Martinis, for the most part, stayed put in steerage. Raffaela was ill for only a few days, but Alberto (17), Elvedio (13), Eraldo (9), and Almerinda (8) practically spent the entire voyage in bed or not feeling well. They seldom went on deck to enjoy the fresh air and ocean spray and never seemed to get accustomed to the rocking back and forth. Typically, when they were not sick or trying to eat, the swaying of their vessel allowed them to sleep the days and nights away in relative comfort.

Perry would have Mario with him every day on the main deck. They would gather two deck chairs and find a spot on the left side or the right side and spend their days talking and eating the large chunks of chocolate and cheese along with fresh bread from steerage. There were a few days of bad weather and they would wander inside, sneaking in and out of areas that were off-limits to steerage passengers. Since Mario was young and small, he could pass as Perry's son; so, most everyone didn't bother with the handsome-looking dad trying to show the boat to his little boy.

One morning, Mario asked a question he had previously posed on their departure.

"Perry, what is this boat called? You promised me you would tell me but you forgot!"

"Mario, this boat is named after a famous Italian explorer named Cristoforo Colombo. Papa and the older men at the cheese factory told me all about him."

"Where was he from in Italy? Rivisondoli?"

Perry chuckled. "No, Mario, I think he was from Genoa, a large seaport in Northern Italy. I am told he actually discovered America."

"What's 'discovered' mean?"

"He found it after sailing on this very ocean."

"Perry, I'm confused. Was America lost?"

Perry laughed again and realized he had to tell Mario the entire story. "No, it wasn't lost. Colombo received permission and money from the Queen of Spain and took a couple of small boats on the Atlantic Ocean. He was searching for land that no one knew existed. People back then thought the world was flat and that he would ultimately fall off the edge of the world when he ran out of water to sail. He landed in America and people from Europe starting settling in this land. Over the years it became a place of hope for many people just like us. And before you ask, that's exactly why we are on this boat and going to America!"

"Oh, but you are scaring me. Will we fall off the edge on the other side?"

"No. Don't be silly. When we get there, we're going to get off and finally see Papa and our brother Giuseppe. Then we're going to live in our new house and never have to work again!"

Mario started to get weepy again. He was born eight months after his dad departed Italy. He had never set eyes on this man he heard so much about who was his father. Anxiety overcame him and he wasn't quite sure why. Perry tried to divert his attention elsewhere.

"Mario, look at how the ocean picks up the waves and splashes foam high in the air."

"Perry, when the waves go back and forth so much, how come the boat just doesn't tip over and push *us* off the edge of the world?"

"Mario, a lot smarter people than us built this boat and I don't think it would tip over no matter what happens. We heard about the great big boat called the *Titanic* that sank a long time ago, but it hit an iceberg way up in the Northern Atlantic Ocean. We're not anywhere near the icebergs, so don't worry." He realized immediately that mentioning icebergs was a mistake.

"Are you sure there are no icebergs near us?"

"Yes, Mario, I'm sure. Don't worry."

Mario returned to what had been on his mind the past thirty minutes.

"Perry, tell me about our father. What is he really like?"

Perry had thought about his papa every single day since his 1920 departure. He was only ten, and his papa had been away either in America or fighting for Italy in World War I for nearly half of his decade of life. He missed him terribly now because his father had not been around during his formative years when he truly became a man. He often thought about Vincenzo never knowing *his* own father. He recalled a conversation he had with his papa right before his last departure for the New World.

"Perry, I know it is difficult for you to understand, but your brother Giuseppe and I must go to America to make arrangements for Mamma, you, and your brothers and sister to join us. There is much hope in my heart that we will have a better life but we must experience and sacrifice this separation first before we are again reunited."

"Papa, I understand, but I don't like it. Why can't I come with you and Joe?"

"It is not possible. We have barely enough money for the two of us to make the crossing, and besides, you are too young to work over there to help, but here in the hills and valleys, you can help Mother."

"Papa, how long will it be before we can come to America?"

"I can't predict that but can only tell you it will not be right away. I am hopeful that before you turn twelve you will be in a place called Ohio."

"Why do we have to go there? Why can't we all stay here and work together in Italy? We're poor but we're all happy. I love it here and just don't understand why we have to move so far away!"

"Perry, Perry, ever the curious and thoughtful son. You know I have traveled to America four times, and on each visit I came to understand that there is no way we will ever experience the kind of freedom and prosperity that exists in that magical place."

Vincenzo continued, "America has literally opened its gates to welcome many of us who are searching and hoping for a better life. I have sailed past what is called the Statue of Liberty when entering this "gate." It's situated in New York Harbor and you too will see it someday. *Figlio mio*, you won't be able to understand the words on the statue, but on my last crossing, I was able to read it and understand it."

Perry remembered leaning forward so he could hear Papa's raspy and soft-spoken voice describe the statue's words.

"Give me your tired and poor yearning to breathe free," his dad would proclaim. "I lift my lamp beside the golden door."

Perry had now realized what a defining moment this had been and now his youngest brother, Mario, was asking him to describe their papa. Someone he had yet to meet.

"Mario, our papa is a great man whom you will come to love immediately. He had a vision many years ago that he would be living in America with his entire family, even before he met Mamma. His gift will be to give us great opportunities to live free and to prosper. In a few days, we will together see the vision of a statue in a harbor right before we get off this boat. I will tell you more as we approach the end of our voyage so you can truly know your papa as I have come to know and remember him. Okay?"

"Perry, what's a statue?"

"It's getting late and the sun is starting to disappear over the horizon. *Andiammo*, come on, let's go down to steerage and join the others for dinner. Remember, pretend you're hungry and eat because Mamma will be upset that I have been feeding you chocolate all day up here on deck!"

"All right. I'll try and eat but the food downstairs stinks!"

Perry and little Mario spent the next two weeks on the main deck eating cheese, chocolate, and fresh bread from steerage. They shared in the delight of the mighty ocean below them while enjoying the scenery of the blue skies and magnificent cloud formations. The older brother repeated stories of the past and they talked about their hopes for the future. The stories captivated Mario's imagination and filled him with delight. One late afternoon, he shook Perry, who had been taking a quiet nap in the fresh breeze.

"Perry, look! A big bird! Where did that huge thing come from?"

Perry awoke suddenly from a dream he was having about making cheese in Italy. Startled by the sight of a rather large seagull, he ran over to an older Italian man and asked him why this bird was so far out to sea near the *Cristoforo Colombo*.

"What's the matter with you, young man? Don't you know we enter the New York Harbor tomorrow morning?"

Mario heard these words and ran down the ladder leading to steerage to tell his family the good news. Perry this time was following Mario.

LESSONS OF LIFE

1. Have courage when entering the unknown.

2. Serve others above self.

3. Love your family.

4. Always entertain hope.

Chapter Four

The Arrival

GIVE ME YOUR TIRED, YOUR POOR, YOUR HUDDLED MASSES,
YEARNING TO BREATHE FREE. THE WRETCHED REFUSE OF YOUR
TEEMING SHORE. SEND THESE, THE HOMELESS, TEMPEST-TOST,
TO ME. I LIFT MY LAMP BESIDE THE GOLDEN DOOR.

- EMMA LAZARUS, STATUE OF LIBERTY

On the morning of their arrival, there was quite the commotion on the outer decks of the *Cristoforo Colombo*, and Perry, with his young brothers, sister, and mother in tow, ran topside to see what all the fuss was about. The ship was at capacity and nearly all were Italian-born. A well-dressed Italian man who had been known to be on his fourth passage yelled with excitement.

"*Guarda, la bella signora. Sulla destra!*" "Look at the beautiful lady. Over there to the right!"

There, rising above the din of the morning haze was the statue they all had come to understand guarded the gateway of the new land. As the ship approached the Statue of Liberty and

Ellis Island, a large roar erupted, for not only was the long transatlantic journey over but the immigrants felt an overwhelming feeling of joy at finally seeing the Great Lady of Promise up close.

Finalmente.

Perry hugged his mother and asked her why she was crying.

"Perry, I haven't seen your papa in five and a half years. What do you think? I've dreamt of this day for many years."

Although he could not read or comprehend the words, Perry stared pensively at the statue and the spectacular greeting of promise she gave: "Give me your tired, your poor, your huddled masses yearning to breathe free. The wretched refuse of your teeming shore. Send these, the homeless, tempest-tost, to me. I lift my lamp beside the golden door." He was awash in memories of how his papa had experienced and passed on to him this special greeting, first penned by nineteenth-century American poet Emma Lazarus, as did the thousands of immigrants in the decades that preceded him. He whispered softly to himself, "*Grazie, Dio.* Thank you, God."

It was March 29, 1927. My father's compass was no longer adrift in a dream of promise, for the vision of arrival was now complete. There was no way of anticipating what was to come. The future already looked bright and promising.

Ellis Island was a sea of mass confusion. It had already become known to many immigrants as the "Island of Tears." Although the Martini family was anxious to reunite with Vincenzo, the lines were backed up everywhere and officials were barking instructions in a language they could not understand. Dad strained to find his own papa and, with great concern, led the family through the lines while attempting to understand the questions posed during the rather abrupt inquisition. Fortunately, fellow Italians in line helped translate the questions with their short, broken-English responses. "Stand over here, stand over there, answer their questions or they'll return you to Italy," they snapped with authority as if directing cattle. Though the family's transatlantic papers were in order, officials isolated them following a four-hour interrogation in the island's holding area behind a large and imposing barbed wire fence. There, they waited impatiently for Papa, who had the required proof of the family's existence in his jacket pocket. They were personally experiencing first hand the "Island of Tears."

As day turned to dusk, interpreters informed them that they should expect to re-board the *Cristoforo Colombo* and return to Italy shortly. Panic stricken, they searched outside the fences in vain to see if they could locate their papa. Perry and his older brother Alberto were ten and eleven when Vincenzo left

Rivisondoli in 1920 and now, as young adults, had the best recollection of his appearance among their brothers and sister.

Alberto pulled on Perry's arm. "Hey, let's go find our papa."

Perry saw him first and recognized his diminutive and quick gait from afar. Screaming "*Papa*" at the top of his lungs, he clutched his dad's fingers through the fence with tears of joy. He was stunned by his dad's sudden appearance.

"Papa, why weren't you here to greet us when we disembarked?" Perry exclaimed through his excitement.

"Perry and Alberto, I didn't receive the telegram until yesterday and have traveled all day and night by train to get here to greet you. Don't despair; we will be on the train heading to our new home soon."

Perry heard his papa's words and wondered aloud, "*Nuova casa?*"

Fear had dreadfully fallen upon them as they awaited deportation at the end of this very long day in March of 1927. Following a roller coaster of emotions, determination and hope outweighed their despair and their reunion with Vincenzo far exceeded the earlier ordeal of their morning arrival in New York Harbor. It was a defining moment of their journey.

Before long, the Martini family boarded a ferry to the mainland and then a motorbus to Penn Station. At the huge rail station, they boarded a train heading further west as their passenger car moved out of the station for an Ohio destination. Mario was wedged in between his brother Perry and father Vincenzo.

"Papa, how much further?" Mario asked, a typical question for a five-year-old as the train had barely made it out of New York City. Almerinda, now eight years old and sitting next to her mamma, turned around and said, "Mario, your papa and brother are sleeping. Close your eyes and we will be there soon."

Brothers Alberto (17), Elvedio (13), and Eraldo (9) were huddled nearby across the aisle and sound asleep. The gentle clacking of the railroad car had placed them in a deep slumber much like the rocking and rolling on the Atlantic, but seasickness was now only a bad memory.

Sleep deprived but excited, they finally arrived in the early morning hours at their destination and new home in Warren, Ohio. They walked from the train's arrival platform the two miles to their new big American house on First Street. It seemed fitting to Perry after walking the hills of Italy, catching a train to Naples to board the passenger ship, making a long journey by sea, and taking a motorbus to the New York train station, that they were now *walking* the last few steps of their trip. Walking was his primary means of transportation in his native land—after all, he spent months shepherding flock in the valleys.

"Papa," Perry asked, "How big is our new house? Is brother Joe waiting for us at the new house? How much further do we have to walk?"

"Perry, aren't you tired? You ask a lot of questions. When I last saw you, we were celebrating your tenth birthday in Italy and I was getting ready to leave for America. You've changed a lot, but that's to be expected. In a few years, it will seem like we always lived here. You'll see."

Now, Perry was stepping briskly alongside his papa and was filled with utter joy to finally be with his hero and leader.

My dad, Perry, recounted on numerous occasions that the memory of seeing their American home was as powerful and as memorable as the first sight of the Statue of Liberty. It is hard for me to imagine my dad's surprise to find that the living room of this new house was larger than their entire bungalow in Italy! "*La casa magnifica!*" It wasn't until I made my first visit to Rivisondoli in 1970 that I fully comprehended the true emotion that ran through my father's veins on seeing his first American "*casa.*" Their Italian home was indeed a small shack: two rooms, no running water, a wood-burning stove that served as both a heater during the harsh winters as well as a single cooking area for family dinners, and one large double bed in the back room with a trundle below for the seven children.

Mamma was impressed with the magnificent garden her husband and son had started in their backyard. Tomatoes, zucchini, lettuce of all types, turnips, eggplant, and beans were in full bloom a few weeks after moving in. Everyone had to get used to using the bathroom "inside" rather than "outside" the house. Vincenzo had purchased new dress clothes for all of them as a welcome home gift. One Sunday morning in May 1927, they dressed up for Sunday Mass and then walked triumphantly over to a local portrait studio for an official family photo. The children were all lined up in order of age and they experienced for the first time ever having their picture taken. It was to be a family photo of their arrival to the American shores and a lasting legacy.

When they returned to their home, they were treated to a wonderful feast of pasta, rolled meats, and fruit and nuts. No one said anything during the meal for they ate heartily and with joy. Vincenzo personally poured them all a glass of local red wine.

He sat up straight in his chair, and with raised glass, said, "*Bienvenuti*, welcome home, and may God bless us all for now we can hope together for a great life of prosperity here in America."

He wept uncontrollably for he was overwhelmed by the reality of what he had prayed for and sacrificed for nearly six years, which now came to a fitting conclusion before his very eyes.

Later that evening, Perry and his brothers and sister were in their rooms on the second floor changing from their Sunday clothes into something a little more comfortable. He heard a commotion downstairs at the front door. He peered out the open window from his room and looked directly down at the front door. There, in the din of the entrance light was a man in a white suit and a large white-brimmed hat. The well-dressed gentleman at the door looked up and took off his hat.

"Perry, why are you standing at the window? Get your Italian butt down here!"

Perry was startled and for a split second he found himself speechless.

"*Zio Giuseppe*! What are you doing here?"

"Perry, are you going to ask questions or get your brothers and sister and come down here and give your favorite uncle a hug?"

Joe Ferrara had surprised them all. He was making his last scouting trip before moving his wife and son to America. He had married Nicolo Daltorio's sister, Concetta, in Rivisondoli some years back, and their son, cousin Guido, was one of the last relatives Perry had said goodbye to before leaving their village.

It was quite the surprise and it dawned on Perry as he lay awake in bed that night exactly what Uncle Giuseppe had meant when he said, "See you soon," during his speedboat farewell in Naples Bay.

Poverty and hard times followed the Martini family to this "land of prosperity" and, although it was devastating for the vast majority of Americans, immigrants were in fact well prepared to handle the adversity. Italians in the 1900s were familiar with poverty. Perry seized the opportunity to use his austere childhood history to overcome insurmountable obstacles. He knew early on that it was best to be calm and patient, to observe closely how others handled their problems, and to keep the wheels of motivation and optimism moving forward. Regardless of the size of the obstacle or the bleakness of the situation, nothing seemed insurmountable to *my* father.

In the early 1930s, the family settled into a rigorous routine of making a house a home. Anyone who was of age found jobs working for minimum wage, primarily in the steel mills. The two oldest brothers, Joe and Albert, married, and my dad found himself the primary provider when his papa became ill. The battle wounds from World War I never quite healed and Vincenzo Martini was in a fight for his life as various stages of respiratory maladies frequented his body with a vengeance starting in 1932.

Meanwhile, Dad became very interested in pursuing a vocation outside of the plants at the local steel mill so he started to learn the barber trade with other Italian immigrants. He completed night school and essentially taught himself to read and write in English. Finally, he was ready to establish a career in the barber business. He asked his dad one evening after dinner if they could talk. After everyone cleared the table, Perry got the nerve to ask his father for some help.

"Dad, I really want to work as a barber, but I cannot increase my clientele without having my own chair. I know we have discussed this in the past and times are tough, but I am trying to get a full-time job at the downtown hotel and without a chair…well…"

His father did not respond but sat quietly contemplating. After a long silence, Vincenzo recognized his son's perseverance and, on a whim, told him he would buy him a barber chair at the local downtown hotel barbershop. Perry saved enough money to make the trip to Cleveland to attend the eight-week barber school. He managed to get by and stayed with friends or relatives and also had a $1 per night bunk at the YMCA for a short time. It was 1934 and the country was now immersed in a deep financial depression. Perry was struggling to help his ailing dad support mother Raffaela and the four remaining teenage siblings who were in various stages of working and night school.

Once established, my dad began to earn a living as a part-time barber but it wasn't enough. As his father's health deteriorated, he started dabbling in amateur boxing at the local boxing arena, using the stage name of "Pepper Martin," to make additional money for the family. He fought only a few fights, losing all but one match, but his bruised face could not hide his evening ventures and the moneymaking scheme came to an end. His dad said, "*Basta!*" "Enough!"

When the doctors finally informed the family that Vincenzo could no longer be treated, my dad realized that there simply wasn't enough time, money, or medical assistance to save his father. On June 4, 1934, Perry sat on the floor of the living room and, while holding his dad's hand and crying uncontrollably, he watched him die slowly and peacefully of pneumonia in Raffaela's arms. In that moment, Perry was a personal witness to his father's final request. Vincenzo wanted the family to know that, even though they were struggling to remain safe and secure in the new country, he needed their promise that they would remain in America and call it home. Raffaela Martini and son Perry listened intently as Vincenzo Martini told his loving wife: "*Vi domando con tutto mio cuole a per favore di stare qui a la America per la speranza di nostril figlie.*" "I implore you to keep hope alive in the hearts and minds of our soon-to-be-fatherless children and please stay here in America."

He wanted his vision of prosperity and freedom to become a reality for his entire family. He found solace on his deathbed that he was able to enjoy the pleasures of fatherhood for nearly thirty years and that his separation during the war and on trips to America only made him more determined to cherish every day of life. Perry paid close attention to these last words and realized that he now possessed something that his own dad never knew: his father's vision and lasting wishes. The path to prosperity and freedom lay ahead on *my* father's compass.

Vincenzo's compass was always set to true north for he realized prophetically what his vision was from that first visit in 1901. America was indeed a place for his family to prosper and to enjoy the wonderful opportunity God had given him. Perry was determined from this point forward that he would fulfill his father's dying wish and pledged to live out his dad's legacy. After burying his dad, he took numerous steps forward and never looked back. Poor was an understatement and the challenges seemed insurmountable. He spent the remainder of the 1930s working part-time as a barber in one of the downtown hotels, working nights at the steel mill, watching his siblings (with the exception of Mario) get married and leave home, and taking good care of his widowed mother.

Thus, this story is not only from my perspective as a son but also from my father who was truly a son following *his* father's compass.

In 1940, my dad married my mom and started the journey for his own family. Dad was thankful he had survived the American Great Depression. He married his Italian sweetheart, Angelina Pietracatello, affectionately called "Angie," who was from Roccaraso, the sister village of his native Rivisondoli. The country was at peace even though the winds of war permeated the very continent he had left thirteen years earlier. He had no idea that he was about to become a member of the Greatest Generation as America was about to enter a worldwide holocaust of monumental proportions and a threat to freedom throughout the globe.

LESSONS OF LIFE

1. Hope is a powerful value.
2. America stands for freedom and prosperity.
3. Assimilate as an immigrant—become a true American.
4. Liberty knows nothing but victories.

Chapter Five

My Father's Compass

NEVER IN THE FIELD OF HUMAN CONFLICT WAS SO MUCH
OWED BY SO MANY TO SO FEW.

                                - WINSTON CHURCHILL, 1940

Americans who were alive on December 7, 1941, are able to recall in minute detail where they were and what they were doing when the news spread throughout the globe that the U.S. Navy Fleet was assaulted by Japanese attack planes. The great conflagration known as World War II was well underway in most of Europe in the late 1930s as the Nazi leader, Adolf Hitler of Germany, and his closest ally, Benito Mussolini of the Fascist party, led Italy. America now faced the ultimate challenge as the eyes of the world turned to the east and west to see how the relatively newly formed America would now react.

My dad, Perry, was not alone as an Italian-born American in feeling not only genuine concern but also disgust regarding the events unfolding in Southern Europe. He, like so many Italian immigrants in the 1920s and 1930s, had escaped abject poverty and the fascist movement that was spreading almost infectiously throughout his native Italy. Nary had a week gone by without someone in the immigrant community receiving disturbing news of family and friends in the old country facing challenges caused by oppressive leaders. These despicable characters were creating havoc among the populace and causing great economic and political strife. Dad's consternation was a feeling of remorse that he couldn't return to Italy and take everyone he knew back to the country he now called home. Nevertheless, the U.S. was immersed in its own crisis in the 1930s, as unemployment, long bread lines, and shortages of all types were common, especially in the middle and lower class structure.

In 1941, Dad had been married over a year, moved into a new home with his wife, started to earnestly consider starting a family, and was finally settling into a new job at the local steel mill. He also was formulating a vision to become a full-time barber but that idea was placed on hold until he had enough capital to open his own shop. Then the news came of the attack on Pearl Harbor and shockwaves reverberated across the continent. President Roosevelt declared war on Japan and shortly thereafter we entered the war in Europe against the Nazi war machine. It was ironic now that a world war was putting *my dad's* vision on hold much like his own dad's during World War I in 1916.

In the aftermath of the war declarations, Americans relied on getting the news through print media and radio. They did not have the benefit of instant cable news or an electronic medium that enabled information to be delivered in a timely manner. But in the first few months of 1942, it became apparent that America was indeed in for the long haul and that many would be called to duty in the armed services as the news trickled to the streets. Mobilization was the buzzword of the day. Dad knew deep down in his gut that it was just a matter of time as the U.S. Government began to accept a multitude of volunteers and to crank up the draft. Rumors were causing confusion and concern among the European immigrant communities as America lined up on the side *opposite* Germany and Italy. Moreover, there were rumors, albeit all true, that Japanese-born Americans were being shuttled off into internment camps on the West Coast, and Italian and German immigrants sensed they were next.

Little has been published regarding Italian internment camps but there were communities in the U.S. that discriminated against Italians. In isolated cases, men were given extended leaves of absence from their jobs, homes were vandalized, and a few families were even imprisoned as alleged European spies. Fortunately, the boroughs in Ohio and

Pennsylvania did not join in the witch-hunt and Dad began to try to find a path to serve his new country.

It was later in 1942, following the birth of his daughter Marie, that he realized he was going to have to leave his home again—only this time it was going to be for a noble cause and service to his new country. Two of his younger brothers, Elvedio and Eraldo, were drafted and joined the Army. Approaching my dad at a welcome home party for my sister after her birth, Elvedio anxiously gave him the news.

"Perry, Eraldo and I have been drafted and we are both joining the Army. I don't think they'll send either of us to the European theater, so, I suspect we are both headed for the Pacific. Perhaps you are old enough to avoid all this, but if I were you, I'd consider joining soon so you can select a service of your choice. I'm worried but I am confident this will all be over soon."

My dad responded in typical fashion.

"Elvedio, please break the news to Mom gently for she is very worried about all of us having to go to war. She still has nightmares of losing her husband because of World War I."

"All right, Perry. That's a good idea."

"I'll take your advice to heart and look into joining but I can't be certain what I'll do. I may not be eligible since I have a wife, daughter, and our mother living with me.

"It bothers me that you and Eraldo have to depart, but we must all do what is necessary to fight for what we came here for. I'm proud of you and Eraldo and will comfort Mom after you give her the news."

Like most European immigrants who were of age to fight, Dad's brothers were told to expect orders to head for the Pacific and Asian theaters. Youngest brother Mario was living in Kent, Ohio, and attending Kent State University while living with extended family from his mother's side of the family—the Ferraras. He entered the Navy Reserve Officer Training Corps (ROTC) program and would eventually become a lighter than air pilot flying blimps for the U.S. Navy. The lone sister, Almerinda, married a Cleveland boy before the war, a first generation Italian-American born by the name of John DiPompei.

Dad's official draft notice arrived, as expected, in late 1942 and he discovered he was going to be inducted into the U.S. Navy and did not need to join. Uncle Sam made the decision for him. He heard rumors that he would end up in the Pacific Ocean on a ship but had no idea as to the details. It's difficult to imagine the atmosphere of anxiety and fear that permeated the United States in early 1942 when reality set in that the country could no longer avoid involvement in this world conflict. Moreover, the mindset of those who emigrated from Asian and

European countries that were directly responsible for starting the global mess must have been seriously conflicted. Dad recalled years later that, as an Italian-born American, the fears of war were compounded with terrifying possibilities of deportation, fighting his own native countrymen, or even serious injury or death in combat. He couldn't help but reflect on the World War I telegram in 1917 when news of his father's death had been nothing but a bad rumor.

When I was a junior in high school, I started to seriously consider my dream of becoming a Navy pilot. In so doing, the U.S. Naval Academy loomed large as a place I wanted to attend if I could somehow qualify for entrance. I bounced my ideas off Dad and it opened up a subject we barely ever discussed. "Dad, I'm thinking about following in Uncle Mario's shoes and becoming a Navy Pilot. I am going to see what it takes to get into the Naval Academy. Uncle Mario thinks I have a chance but wants me to consider Navy Reserve Officer Training Corps (NROTC) if I can't qualify for the Academy. What do you think?"

"Perry, you know how I feel about the Navy. My experience during World War II was positive and truly gave me a chance to understand why your grandfather had a vision to come to America. Do you know what I think about often regarding the Great War?"

"No, Dad, *dirme.*" "Tell me."

"It was dreadful in 1942 when I realized I may have to go off to war. I couldn't get out of my mind that my father died at the age of 54 because of a war wound he received fighting for Italy. Can you imagine leaving home with your mom, sister, and grandmother hanging onto me at the train station?"

I saw him fighting back the tears, so I quickly interrupted him. "No, Dad, it's hard for me to imagine."

Much has been written about the men and women who served in the Great War. They are appropriately referred to as the "Greatest Generation," not only for their heroic duty and service to the defense of liberty and freedom of America, but also for their selfless contribution to world peace. Their individual patriotic heroism will most likely never be replicated. Today, many who served and survived the worldwide war continue to die at an alarming rate of well above 1,000 per day. Soon, we will no longer have them among us, and yet their legacy will live on as they set the standard of greatness and true servant leadership during the 20th century.

The world was a mess in the late 1930s in both Europe and the Far East. Adolf Hitler was wreaking havoc politically beyond the borders of Germany and using brunt military power to overpower the will of the citizens of Czechoslovakia, Italy, and Poland, and many other neighbor governments, and was scheming to overtake England and Russia. As elected leader of the Nazi party, he convinced the Germans that they were the superior race and must eliminate anyone who stood against them in promoting the Arian race. Moreover, he personally decided to extinguish the Jewish population of Europe, which led to what we now know as the Holocaust. Another dictator, Benito Mussolini, who was concurrently convincing Italians that they needed to embrace Fascism in alliance with Nazism, joined him.

Meanwhile, the Japanese leadership was plotting to rule the globe through Imperialism and, in 1941, successfully attacked the U.S. Navy fleet in Pearl Harbor, Hawaii, forcing the Americans to declare War on Japan on December 8, 1941. A day later, Germany declared war on the U.S. and World War II began in earnest for the United States in both the European and Pacific theaters. Three years later, the U.S. and its allies brought the Axis Powers to their knees in defeat and sued for peace. Millions were wounded and killed in this worldwide conflagration and the United States mourned the loss of over 300,000 soldiers, sailors, airmen, and marines.

Dad received his first set of orders in 1942 following boot camp to report to the *USS Rocky Mount*, a Navy communications ship ported in Pearl Harbor, affectionately referred to by her crew as "The Rock." During the next two years, he floated around the Western and Southern Pacific unknowingly avoiding Japanese attack aircraft and enemy submarines. His ship was attacked very few times since their mission was to position themselves as a communications relay platform over the horizon away from the main battle groups. The *USS Rocky Mount* was a high-value target since it was the flagship of Admiral Kinkaid, USN, Commander of the Seventh Fleet, and also carried Admiral Turner, USN, Commander of the Pacific Amphibious Forces. Nevertheless, she was able to employ tactics to avoid detection and maintain the highest level of secrecy as to her whereabouts.

Dad never received any war medals or commendations directly related to combat. He humbly served as a dedicated Barbers Mate and as a member of the ship's personnel service department. He did what he did best—served others. Sure, he spent many frightful hours manning the gun mounts during General Quarters (GQ) when attack aircraft or submarines were in their general vicinity, but he spent most of his time helping his fellow crewmembers live comfortably in between moments of stark terror.

While Dad was running a fifteen-chair barbershop onboard the Rock, the war in the Pacific was escalating from 1942 through 1943; Guadalcanal, Leyte Gulf, Iwo Jima, Solomon and Aleutian Islands, and other campaign victories became synonymous with American and Allied success. Dad knew little of these great battles but learned from the senior officers onboard the Rock that American wherewithal was defeating the Japanese and that the war would end soon.

Dad was popular among the officers and chiefs and they waited patiently in his barbershop to have him personally cut their hair. Dad was always willing and able to carry on an interesting conversation with his "customers" and this communication skill was to become one of his greatest strengths as a barber. He listened carefully and closely observed his leaders and was always looking for someone to emulate and follow. He quickly became a leader in his shop and was well liked by other service personnel on the mess decks and personnel divisions. The chiefs promoted him to Petty Officer Third Class and placed him in a leadership position. For good reason he became very popular among the crew during his thirty months on the Rock.

It is important to note that Dad's contribution to the war effort was his simple caring heart in providing service to others. He knew inherently that people didn't care what he knew but knew that he cared. He was a constant morale booster for he knew how adversity could get in the way of optimism. He went out of his way to encourage others to believe that the war would be over soon and they would be reunited with their families.

Deep down, he worried about his brothers who were somewhere in the war, and he wrote frequently to his wife, who would pass on his love to his mother, Raffaela, who was living with her back in Warren, Ohio. His mom prayed constantly for the safe return of her sons. She prayed for Italy to be safe for she still had many family members in Rivisondoli and hoped they would be spared from the bombing that was taking place throughout Europe. Dad instinctively knew of his mother's concerns and was forever comforting her through his letters by giving her much to hope for in the way of an eventual peace. He was one of millions who hoped and prayed for a quick ending in 1943, but much was yet to be accomplished on the war front.

My dad was one among the many who quietly served his country in the defense of freedom and liberty but would never consider himself a hero. On the other hand, there were those who became well known for their incredible heroics and garnered national recognition for their distinguished contribution to the war effort. One such man was Lieutenant Commander Butch O'Hare. I wrote about him in my latest book, *Inspiring Leadership: Character and Ethics Matter*, because of his courageous actions in the South Pacific Theater during World War II and his commitment to inspiring so many others to follow in his footsteps. Fittingly, this war hero followed *his* father's compass and legacy and would speak about his character and courage among his fellow warriors.

Upon his graduation from the United States Naval Academy in 1937, Butch received his Navy "Wings of Gold" following intensive training in Pensacola, Florida, and was subsequently assigned as a fighter pilot on the aircraft carrier *Lexington* in the South Pacific. It is important to share his story and to show how he followed his father's compass.

Following a frantic carrier launch during World War II, Butch looked at his fuel gauge after he was airborne and realized that someone had forgotten to top off his fuel tank. Since he would not have enough fuel to complete his mission and get back to his ship, his flight leader told him to return to the carrier. Reluctantly, Butch dropped out of formation and headed back to the fleet.

As he was returning to the *Lexington*, he saw something that turned his blood cold. A squadron of nine Japanese aircrafts was speeding its way toward the American fleet. The American fighters were already gone on a sortie and the fleet was all but defenseless. He couldn't reach his squadron and bring them back in time to save the fleet; nor could he warn the fleet of the approaching danger. There was only one thing to do: divert the squadron of attack planes from the fleet.

Laying aside all thoughts of personal safety, Butch dove into the formation of Japanese planes. Wing-mounted .50 calibers blazed as he charged in and attacked one surprised enemy plane and then another. Butch weaved in and out of the now broken formation and fired at as many planes as possible until, finally, all his ammunition was spent. Undaunted, he continued the assault. He dove at the planes, trying to at least clip off a wing or tail in hopes of damaging as many enemy planes as possible. He was desperate to do anything he could to keep them from reaching the American ships.

Finally, the two remaining exasperated Japanese aircraft took off in another direction. Deeply relieved, Butch O'Hare and his tattered fighter limped back to the carrier. Upon arrival, he reported in and related the event surrounding his return. The film from the camera mounted on his plane told the tale and showed the extent of Butch's daring attempt to protect his fleet. He had destroyed seven enemy aircraft.

This heroic feat was accomplished on February 20, 1942, and, for that action, Butch O'Hare became the Navy's first ace of World War II and the first naval aviator to win the Medal of Honor. A great man and a great story about courage and true character.

Another story about character and courage took place in Chicago in the 1930s about a man named "Easy Eddie." During the Great Depression, gangster boss Al Capone virtually owned this city. Capone wasn't famous for anything heroic and his exploits were anything but praise-worthy. He was, however, notorious for enmeshing the city of Chicago in everything from booze to prostitution to murder.

Easy Eddie was Capone's lawyer and for a good reason: he was very good. In fact, his skill at legal maneuvering kept Big Al out of jail for a long time. To show his appreciation, Capone paid Eddie very well and gave him special dividends. In fact, Easy Eddie and his family occupied a fenced-in mansion with live-in help and all of the conveniences of the day. The estate was so large that it filled an entire Chicago city block. Eddie lived the high life of the Chicago Mob and gave little consideration to the atrocities that went on around him.

However, Eddie did have one soft spot: a son that he loved dearly. Eddie saw to it that his young son had the best of everything from clothes to cars to a good education. Nothing was withheld and price was no object. Furthermore, despite his involvement with organized crime, Eddie even tried to teach his son right from wrong in hopes of raising him to be a better man than he was himself. Yet, with all his wealth and influence, there were two things that Eddie couldn't give his son, two things that Eddie sacrificed to the Capone Mob that he could not pass on to his beloved son: a good name and a good example. His son wanted him to divest himself from this sordid life and begged him for some direction in life that he could follow.

One day, Easy Eddie reached a difficult decision. Offering his son a legacy, a father's compass, was far more important than all the riches he could lavish on him. He had to rectify all the wrong that he had done. He would go to the authorities and tell the truth about "Scarface" Al Capone. He would try to clean up his tarnished name and offer his son some semblance of integrity.

To do this he would have to testify against the Mob and he knew that the cost would be great. But, more than anything, he wanted to be an example to his son. He wanted to do his best to make restitution and hopefully have a good name to leave his son. So, he testified. Within the year, Easy Eddie's life ended in a blaze of gunfire on a lonely Chicago street. He had given his son the greatest gift he had to offer at the greatest price he would ever pay.

What do these two stories of character and courage have to do with one another?

Butch O'Hare was Easy Eddie's son.

Butch returned from the war to eulogize his fallen father and spoke only of his dad's moral courage and true character in doing the right thing. A few years later, Butch was killed in aerial combat at the age of 29 in Tarawa in the South Pacific. His hometown would not allow the memory of that heroic action to die. Today, O'Hare Airport in Chicago is named in tribute to the courage of this great man.

Butch O'Hare, World War II Ace and Medal of Honor winner, was a product of his father's legacy and served his country knowing his dad passed down to him the example of integrity and honor. Another son who was proud of his dad and followed his father's compass spent years in a POW camp in Vietnam. Senator John McCain was suffering horribly because his father was the Commander of U.S. Forces in the Pacific and those who held him captive never let him forget it. He wrote in his book, *Faith of My Fathers*, that when Vietnamese military officers realized he was indeed the son of a top commander, they offered him a chance for an early release in an effort to embarrass the United States. Acting from a sense of integrity and honor taught by his father, he refused the offer. He was tortured, held in solitary confinement, and imprisoned for five and a half years following this refusal, but he never wavered from his father's compass.

James Bradley's father, John "Doc" Bradley, was one of the six flag raisers at Iwo Jima. His book, *Flags of our Fathers*, is an epic look at a generation at war and its aftermath. He writes extensively about the fact that his dad hardly ever spoke of the famous photo or about his coincidental place in history. James

Bradley learned that his father's compass was truly focused on paying homage to those who were the true heroes of Iwo Jima. Before he died, he told his son, "The real heroes of Iwo Jima were the guys who didn't come back."

My dad's contribution to the war effort never made it to the pages of history but, nevertheless, it was much more the norm of those who were members of the Greatest Generation. Dad had truly become a servant leader among his peers in his own quiet way and he was able to reflect on the lessons of his father's example of perseverance, loyalty, humility, and integrity. Vincenzo's compass clearly provided the course to follow for his entire family and Dad was able to hang onto those unmistaken values and beliefs that provided the necessary motivation to love his family, his country, and his fellow man. His patriotism was formed from his love of home and, although he never forgot his Italian roots, he served in the war protecting those very privileges of freedom and liberty that attracted and brought him and his family to America in the first place.

A compass is an instrument used by countless humans who are searching for the direction that will align them with a purpose. Navigators for centuries have found their way by knowing the magnetic bearing of true north. It has provided accurate information for one to set a course—to head in a certain and precise direction. Similarly, my father knew he had to stay focused on the goal and press on with the destination in mind. Much like his father who had passed away over twelve years prior to the end of World War II, he set his course for the future and was determined not to let anything get in the way of his love for family and his plans for the future.

He returned to Warren, Ohio, as the war concluded in 1945 amid much jubilation for, in addition to a welcome homecoming with his wife and daughter, he learned that brothers Elvedio, Eraldo, and Mario were all safe and returning home to rejoin their families.

Raffaela knew during this long world conflict all would be well as she relied on her strong and abiding faith that her sons would be protected. She prayed now more than ever that the family could finally focus on being prosperous and fulfilling her late husband's vision.

LESSONS OF LIFE

1. Know your compass and follow it.
2. Serve others above self.
3. Leadership is character in motion.
4. Fight for something worthwhile.

Vincenzo and Raffaela Martini,
reunited in 1927, Warren, Ohio.

Martini children's first portrait following arrival in America,
spring 1927; Left to right, Giuseppe (22), Alberto (18), Perry
(17), Elvedio (13), Eraldo (10), Almerinda (9), and Mario (6).

Martini family portrait, spring 1927; Left to right top row, Elvedio, Perry, Connie (Giuseppe's future wife), Giuseppe, Alberto. Left to right bottom row, Eraldo, Vincenzo, Mario, Raffaela, and Almerinda.

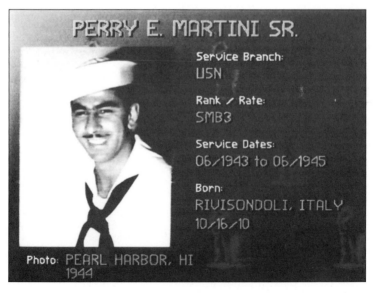

PERRY E. MARTINI SR.

Service Branch:
USN

Rank / Rate:
SMB3

Service Dates:
06/1943 to 06/1945

Born:
RIVISONDOLI, ITALY
10/16/10

Photo: PEARL HARBOR, HI
1944

Navy Memorial Log, Washington, D.C.

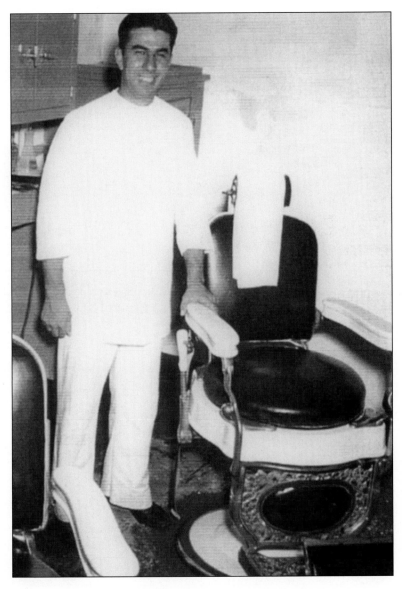

Perry Martini, Sr., first barbershop on Youngstown Road,
Warren, Ohio, June 1948.

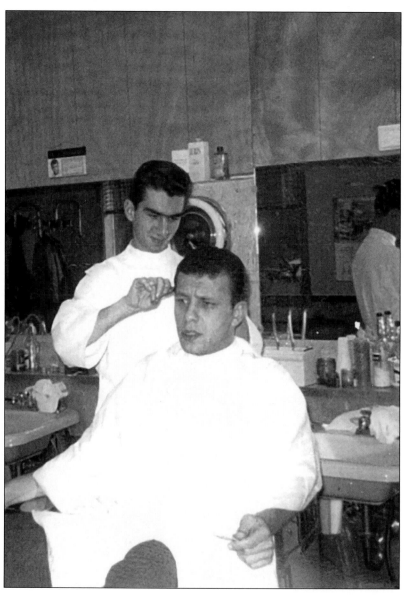

Eraldo (Marty) Martini, Jr., giving fellow barber
Bob Bonnano a haircut, June 1963.

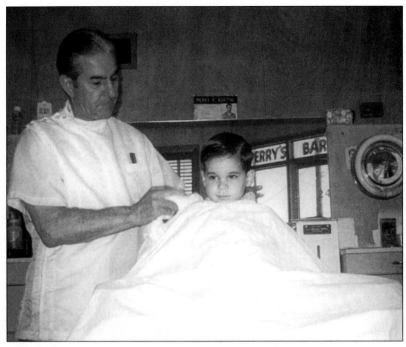

Perry Martini, Sr., giving great-nephew
John Golloway's first haircut, 1970.

Cristoforo Colombo - October 1927

Captain Mario Martini, USNR, 1962.

Perry Martini, Sr., official U.S. Navy photograph upon
entering World War II, Pearl Harbor, HI, June 1943.

Captain Perry J. Martini, Jr., USN, 1992.

Chapter Six

My Father's Vision

WHEN THERE IS NO VISION, THE PEOPLE PERISH.

- PROVERBS 29:18

My father's return from the war turned the page on a new chapter in his life and signaled for him a return to the basics. He was anxious to jumpstart his lifelong vision of settling down with his family and focusing on developing a career that would provide for his family as both a husband and father. Moreover, he wanted to continue to complete his preordained mission and honor his father's final wish to take care of the widowed Raffaela. Dad learned early in life in those few years of school and church training that the only commandant of God that yields a promise is if you "honor thy father and thy mother you will be given the gift of a long and prosperous life." He returned to work in the steel mill in the hot and dirty pickle plant and started to gain the financial capital and emotional momentum necessary in these post-war years to buy a new home and to find a way to open his own business in the barber trade.

Dad had a remarkable ability to look beyond the present. In his own simple way, he was the consummate visionary. Mario, his youngest brother, had experienced a life-defining moment and turning point in his young life that was brought on by Dad's uncanny ability to dream and to project a vision. Mario did not fully comprehend this talent in his older brother until reflecting upon a man-to-man conversation with his older brother that occurred shortly after the passing of their father, Vincenzo.

We return to the story of the Martini family struggling with life in America in the 1930s following the death of Vincenzo Martini.

Mario was the only member of this immigrant family to start elementary school in accordance with his age, although it was a tough start and he spent an extra year in first grade due to language challenges. When he finally entered high school, he was glad he didn't have to endure the pain of childish scorn that his other brothers experienced as teenagers, for example, squeezed into school desk chairs in small elementary school classrooms. Sister Almerinda and brother Eraldo had completed high school but it was not done in the proper sequence of age.

Notwithstanding those few attending school, all of the children were working odd jobs and were able to help their older brother Perry by contributing meager weekly paychecks to assist in maintaining a household and paying the necessary bills of food, clothing, and shelter. Vincenzo had left a vacuum in financial support and it was now Perry's duty to ensure that mother Raffaela could put food on the dinner table and live as comfortably as possible in spite of the surrounding depressed state of the U.S. economy. Mario was no exception as he made money setting duck pins in a local bowling alley (three cents per set-up), peddling newspapers, helping his older brothers paint houses, and working the outfield scoreboard for the local Negro baseball league at a buck a game.

Perry asked Mario to remain at the dinner table one evening in 1937 before proceeding to his room to finish some homework. It was not just a brotherly chat but more along the lines of a father-son discussion.

"Mario, we need to talk about your future as you now enter high school."

"Perry, why talk about that now?" Mario nervously sought to end the conversation for his older brother was quite the taskmaster. "I'm just starting next month."

"You don't understand. You have the potential of someday attending college since your brothers and sister started school here in America too late to have the opportunity."

"Again, Perry, why talk about that now? I still have a long way to go."

"You need to know that Mamma and I have talked and from now on, you won't be required to add your weekly earnings into the family pot. I want you to start saving for college now. *Pronto!*"

"You mean I don't have to contribute to the family fund that provides for food and clothing?"

"Well, not exactly. We'll pay for the food you eat and buy your clothes, but you have to buy your own shoes as you continue to grow."

Mario's head was spinning. "How much can I really save?" he muttered to himself.

Mario was stunned. His dad was no longer in his life and he was still grieving his loss, especially since he hadn't even met him until the "crossing" when he was a mere five years of age. Ten years had passed since he and older brother Perry had huddled together eating chocolate and cheese topside on the *Cristoforo Colombo* and the indescribable anticipation he felt upon finally meeting his papa. How was he to know that there would be so little time for him to be with his father before he died seven short years later? Now, his surrogate father was laying out an opportunity of a lifetime for him and providing him with a personal clear vision. It was a selfless act by Perry who knew he would have to make up for the loss of Mario's weekly income to the family kitty. Mario was anxious but thankful and he began to focus on schoolwork and a college savings plan.

In 1940, Mario was set to graduate from high school. He had successfully saved about $5 a month during his high school years and was ready to accept an offer to attend Kent State University (KSU) located nearby in Kent, Ohio. The plan he presented to Perry was solid: he would live and work with cousins on the Ferrara side of the family who owned and operated a local supermarket. The $375 he saved would pay for two years of college tuition and the work at the cousins' supermarket would provide payment for room and board. His brother Perry was getting ready to marry Angelina, his Ravenna, Ohio, sweetheart whose Roccarosa, Italy, roots were those of the sister town of his own Rivisondoli.

Perry was mighty proud of young Mario for what he managed to accomplish and triumphantly sent him off to KSU and the Ferrara family. Mario completed his first two years of college on his own dime and joined the U.S. Navy in 1942 to fight in the war. He worked his way through the officer and pilot training pipeline and in July of 1943, a few days after his twenty-second birthday, was commissioned an Ensign in the United States Navy. He was assigned to his first duty station as a lighter than air pilot and flew Navy blimps for the remainder of the war until 1946.

Mario took advantage of the U.S. Government's returning veteran scholarship program called the "GI Bill" and was readmitted to KSU in 1947. In 1949, Mario Martini became the only son or daughter of this immigrant family to graduate and receive a college degree. It had been twenty-two years since the "crossing." No one was prouder than his older brother Perry on reaching this pinnacle in life. Deep down, both had come to realize that the vision that was planted during their 1937 conversation was now fulfilled.

The story of Dad's ability to formulate a vision in order to clearly manage the ebb and flow of life's events is clearly illustrated in the success Mario was able to attain through Dad's counsel and mentoring. My dad also took the necessary steps in completing his vision for his own life by settling on the issue of purchasing a home in 1948 and converting this new abode into not only *la casa* but also a place to start his new business.

The vision was now becoming clearer as Perry took the barber chair his father had purchased for him in the 1930s and placed it on the enclosed front porch of his new home. He hung a small sign on the entrance door in June 1948 that simply read, "Perry's Barber Shop." Near the front window he hung a small motionless barber pole to keep with the tradition of the visible symbol that signified that this was indeed a place of business for haircuts, shaves, and other services for the welcome customers. Perry and Angie had made the big move to their new home in early 1948 and, as the move progressed, they anticipated the arrival of two additional family members. Dad moved mother Raffaela, who had been living in Cleveland with Almerinda after the War, back to Warren to live in the new *casa*.

I was born in April and named Perry James Martini, Jr.

And so it was in 1948 that my father experienced a new home, a returning mother, a wife giving birth to his first son, a daughter starting first grade, and a brand new "start-up" business with a barber pole mounted near the front door.

"Next!"

LESSONS OF LIFE

1. Follow your compass—live your vision.

2. Serve others above self.

3. Love your family.

4. Recognize defining moments in life.

Chapter Seven

Servant Leadership: Following One's Compass

The idea of servant leadership is certainly not a new concept. However, many leaders have forgotten how powerful it is and often fail to use it, either through ignorance or arrogance. Robert Greenleaf coined the phrase in modern times in his highly proclaimed 1970 essay, *The Servant as a Leader*. Servant leadership actually goes back thousands of years. There was a history of warrior-spirited leadership that permeated the ancient world that was the style associated with military leaders who led sailors and soldiers into battle as the average citizen struggled for self-governance. Roman and Greek leaders, for example, would have been considered contrary to the concept of servant leadership.

The idea that leaders must put their people before themselves was a radical break with history. Leaders were accustomed to ruling through tyranny and fear. Some ancient philosophers made a mild attempt at this approach but it wasn't until Jesus' appearance on earth that the concept of servanthood took hold. It is apparent that he proscribed to this style in his teachings and written proclamations and billions have followed him since. Today, many consultants, trainers, and college professors teach the premise of this style of leadership to encourage leaders and managers to genuinely care for their people. Many stress to the uninitiated that the servant leader is a servant first. This approach begins with the natural feeling that one wants to serve first, and, eventually, a conscious choice brings one to aspire to lead.

If someone had approached my father in 1948 to discuss the basics regarding servant leadership, he would have been confused by the definitions and verbiage behind the concept. He knew what servant leadership was because it was the way he lived his life. It came naturally to him because his innate instincts and desires were to serve others above himself. As he moved his barber chair from the front porch into the connected commercial building in 1950, it was the beginning of his career as not only a manager of his business but, more importantly, as a leader. Over time, he began to build his business by adding additional barber chairs and hiring barbers.

Dad set up two chairs in the back room of a corner delicatessen that was actually connected to the house via a basement tunnel. He hired his first employee and subsequently opened his "ledger" in the spring of 1950. Without the benefit of a business education, Dad had to consult with friends and fellow barbershop owners and, in doing so, formed a rudimentary business strategy and set in motion an appropriate mission that included a business plan, goals, and objectives. He used his ability as a kind and generous manager to handle the day-to-day service operations of a classic cash flow business.

As I reflect back to all of this and re-read my father's personal barbershop ledger, I am struck by what he was able to do by just observing and learning from others. It is truly remarkable that he could run a business without the benefit of an accounting background or exposure to other helpful information such as a "how-to" book. Today, we might find a book on the shelf at the local bookstore titled *Barber Business for Dummies*, whereas, in 1950, no such handy resource was readily available to someone like my dad.

I naïvely asked my dad about the business when it began to really flourish.

"Dad, how come the barbers really like to work here at your barbershop?"

He didn't respond so I continued, "You know, they seem to always be in a good mood even though all of this seems like a lot of work."

After what seemed like five minutes, he said, "I think my barbers know that I really care about their well-being."

"Where did you learn that this was so important?"

"I learned during the Depression years that I always seemed to work harder and enjoy my job when I worked for bosses who gave a darn about me, my family, and served me as if I were their boss! It worked for me as an employee so I thought it would be beneficial to follow their example when I became the boss."

My dad had figured out by observing others and using them as role models how to become a servant leader by virtue of using his heart and not any head knowledge to manage a well-run barbershop. Servant leadership is not something you can learn from a book; nor can it be faked. It is the highest expression of the human spirit and comes from one's heart. My dad had plenty of this, and he was able to quickly rise above his own self-interest to accommodate the barbers he continued to hire as he expanded his business. His business had grown to four chairs in late 1954 when he moved to the front of the building that formerly housed the delicatessen.

There was also expansion in the household for another son was added to the family as my brother, Vince, who was named after the visionary family patriarch, Vincenzo, was born in November. During this period of growth, Dad and his brothers began to seriously consider constructing an attached apartment for their mother, Raffaela. Unbeknownst to me, this renovation of our home by my dad and uncles was the first exposure for me as a very young boy to a remarkable demonstration of unconditional love and selflessness.

While Dad provided the financial support necessary for materials, four of his brothers, busy raising their own families in Warren, were able to apply their own personal expertise to the project. Dad's oldest brother Joe was a master self-taught electrician. Albert, a carpenter, had the uncanny ability to visualize a construction project and he demonstrated frequently his special talent to create something out of nothing almost single-handedly. Elvedio loved to paint and was always searching to help someone with a paint job. Joe, Albert, and Elvedio all worked in the local steel mills but immensely enjoyed these self-taught skills, especially when helping each other. Their younger brother Eraldo was a tailor by trade but he had developed skills in record keeping and went out of his way to help others with administrative details, including helping my dad by showing him how to audit his own barber business financial ledgers.

Together, these true selfless immigrants and servant leaders completed their mother's apartment in a few months and it was a proud day when she moved down our second floor hallway and entered her new *casa piccola*. It was nearly the same size as the humble abode she left behind in Rivisondoli complete with a kitchen, master bedroom, and a sitting room where she would spend the next three decades crocheting doilies and other fine linens that were proudly displayed in every one of her descendants' homes.

Unremarkably, and in their own way, Dad's brothers exemplified the style of selfless leadership my dad was emulating in his barber business. Their simple methods validated his approach in helping others be successful in working together as a functional team. Servant leaders realize early on that they cannot be successful alone, and that they must count on others to share in not only the effort required, but also, more importantly, in the credit afforded to those deserving for a job well done.

Like the great rivers of the world, servant leaders place themselves below the streams that feed into them. They are generous with one of their most precious resources: time. They offer continuous guidance and encouragement. They manage their followers by walking around in the trenches. They catch people doing a great job and acknowledge it immediately. Dad was good at this, and barbers who worked for him always knew where they stood and had absolute trust in Dad's judgment and decisions.

Servant leaders are also good listeners. They find out their people's needs by asking them directly, then listening with genuine empathy. Most importantly, they act on what they've heard and give constant feedback. This was not my dad's strong suit. He loved and admired all he came in contact with and the one area of weakness that prevailed for Dad was that, while he was short on listening, he would never be at a loss for words once he grabbed the conversation. Actually, he didn't miss anything that was said for he formulated thoughts and shared ideas immediately and was able to quickly connect with customers and friends during periods of verbal engagement.

He was famous behind the barber chair for never giving a silent or boring haircut. Most family members, including myself, saw this loquacious nature as over the top. Admittedly, it was something he had to work at constantly, but it did not stop him from being genuinely concerned for others almost to a fault. Dad had a keen sense of connecting to people he came in contact with and he instinctively understood their belief systems and built trust quickly with them based on their shared personal experiences. He gave everyone the benefit of the doubt based on the value they placed on family, faith, and a strong work ethic. He did not connect well with anyone he perceived to be unpatriotic or unwilling to place their love for family as their most esteemed value. He saw the virtue in people who exhibited a love of life and were upbeat and optimistic. It was common for people to see the genuine kindness in his heart when meeting him for the first time. Over the years, I hardly ever met a person who did not respect and admire my father and this perceived weakness of verbosity was rarely mentioned.

At my dad's funeral, I was struck by the number of people I had never met who came up to me and expressed their admiration for my father. One gentleman who had become a customer of my dad at the young age of five approached me at the wake and said, "I knew your father as a young boy and always admired him. My dad loved your dad as well. Growing up I always looked forward to getting my hair cut by your dad. I have now lost a lifelong friend. I have to tell you that I have never known anyone kinder in my entire life. He always made you feel special and you could always tell by his eyes that he cared about you."

Servant leaders place others above their own self-interest and their moral compass always seems rooted within this highly valued philosophy. It almost always comes down to leadership and one's personal connection to others and is paramount to one's true character. Maintaining a steady course when one is navigating life's ebb and flow is essential to overcoming the turbulence that seems to prevent us from reaching our desired destinations.

The compass is used as an instrument for determining directions by means of a freely rotating magnetic needle that indicates magnetic north. This is the commonly accepted definition when using the word compass as a noun. When used as an adjective, the word communicates something quite different: to attain or achieve. A common theme regarding corporate leadership vis-à-vis a compass emerged from the first two Academy Leadership series books, *The Leader's Compass* (Haley and Ruggero, 2003) and *The Corporate Compass* (Haley and Ruggero, 2005). In *The Leader's Compass*, the authenticity of a leader is validated by a written personal leadership philosophy that outlines the individual's belief system and values as well as a cogent vision and mission statement. In *The Corporate Compass*, an organization affirms that it is focused on its purpose and vision and realigns its stated goals by identifying the values required to support them. Leaders have a proclivity to enjoin followers that will be attracted to the leader's clearly stated direction; ultimately, this should result in the arrival at a common destination. Metaphorically, the leader's compass keeps the leader on course and provides the focus and alignment necessary to not go adrift.

My father's compass kept him on course as a servant leader and provided a constant bearing on his role as the leader of his barbershop. In the 1960s, his now seven-chair shop flourished. In keeping with his value system, he hired barbers who would share his vision of a service-based business that provided not only great haircuts but also a local establishment that customers frequented. As he focused on the values of his own family, it was not a surprise that he hired other descendants of immigrant Italians, including two nephews. Without the benefit of formal training, he nonetheless took on the role of mentoring as he coached these young new employees to learn the trade that he truly loved.

A mentor is one who facilitates the experiential learning that eventually results in future-oriented abilities. The term refers to a person who is a trusted role model, advisor, wise one, friend, steward, or guide—a person who works with emerging human and organizational forces to tap energy and purpose, to shape new visions and plans, and to generate desired results. A mentor is devoted to inspiring an increase in competence, commitment, and confidence in others. The most profound way to garner leadership skills and values is to learn them directly from one who already possesses these qualities and who is willing to share the lessons they have learned. Mentors have specific strengths that they apply to situations and, as leaders, then quickly determine what it takes to facilitate professional development in someone they perceive may have the potential to achieve success.

Dad was devoted to those who worked for him and was especially pleased to have two of his brothers' sons as contemporaries in his barbershop. They were both named after their dads, Albert and Eraldo, and it was a thrill for my father to have them near him on a daily basis. He loved them as a father, as a servant leader, and as a mentor, and he guided them through their apprenticeship to help them work towards achieving a journeyman and master barber status. Again, there was a sense of family with all the barbers working for my dad and this was constantly validated by the many that enjoyed long-term employment at his barbershop. Rather than consider these barbers as his subordinates, he considered them true associates once they worked their way through the required one-year apprenticeship.

I also joined the business as a young man in the early 1960s; however, I use the term "joined" somewhat loosely. As my father had learned early in his adult life in the 1930s, everyone works to support the family in any way possible and his own children were no exception. Naturally, I broached the subject of wages only once and discovered quickly that my non-wage-earning status was helping us put food on the table and to buy nice clothes for school.

"Dad, why can't I receive an allowance for working here in the barber shop? A lot of my buddies receive an allowance for doing chores at home. I do my chores at home *and* work here in the shop, yet don't get paid."

My dad was steamed, and I tensed up as to what might follow. He raised his voice.

"You wear nice clothes to school and church, you get a new pair of shoes every year, you have a nice warm bed to sleep in, and your mom feeds you well when you waltz up to the dinner table!

"You get paid well and don't ever bring it up again!"

This was a tough pill to swallow for a product of the '50s and '60s but the lessons realized in later years certainly made me a better person. I have often reflected on whether I got involved in sports and other afterschool activities because I enjoyed them or because they relieved me of my barbershop duties since I arrived home at quitting time. Regardless, there were many days I appeared at the shop following football practice and found the broom waiting for me near the front door. It was during these years that I was able to observe my father very closely and, although I was very naïve in how to be a manager and run a business, I was always in awe of his decision-making skills and innate ability to ensure customers *and* his barbers were happy campers.

We fondly remember the servant leaders we have known. They had profound impact on our lives and truly molded us and inspired us. In many cases, they were our parents, coaches, teachers, friends, and even our bosses. Ultimately, we sensed their love for us and we returned it in kind. In my case, my father had a major impact on me through the enduring lessons I learned from him, which were a direct result of my father's personal compass.

LESSONS OF LIFE

1. Be a good listener.
2. Encourage others and always be kind.
3. Optimism is contagious.
4. Honor your father and mother.
5. Encourage your children always.
6. Willingly help family and friends in need— give of yourself.
7. Care about others above self-interests.

Chapter Eight

Leadership Lessons for an Immigrant Son

I have a flood of memories that serve as defining moments in my life and lessons passed down from my father. There is not much that occurs in our lives without some effect from our parents, and for me, it set my compass early on and the course was inalterable.

Two life-changing events occurred in the 1960s that will forever be ingrained in the introspection of my formative years that had a bearing on *my* compass. The first such event occurred early one morning in 1964. As was my routine before departing for school, I passed through our connected basement tunnel to bring Dad a morning cup of coffee. I was shocked to find my cousin, Marty, hovered over my dad near the entrance to the barbershop. Marty was pulling Dad's tongue out of his throat to prevent him from choking to death.

"Perry, I'm worried that your dad can't breathe. It looks like he had a heart attack."

I came upon them quickly and dropped the cup of coffee. It took a few seconds for Marty's words to sink in.

"I'll call an ambulance. *Subito!*"

Apparently, Dad had passed out a few minutes prior to our near simultaneous arrival on the scene; unbeknownst to either one of us, he was actually experiencing a mild stroke at the young age of fifty-four. Dad was hospitalized for a few days of observation, recovered at home in less than two weeks, and was back on the job a short time later. The doctors were not sure why the stroke had been brought on but assured everyone that Dad would be fine. He lived on for over thirty years hence and, notwithstanding some short bouts with congestive heart failure, there was never a reoccurrence of a serious illness or hospitalization. During his absence, the shop ran smoothly without him as he was always in the mentor mode ensuring he was not indispensable as a manager of a seven-chair barbershop. It was a testimony to his leadership skills and how he set the example for others to follow.

When he had been released from the hospital and arrived back at the house for bed rest, we had a quiet moment together.

"Perry, I thought a lot these past few days about your grandfather, Vincenzo, dying at the young age of fifty-four. It occurred to me just how much I missed him and how I had to live without a dad for many years. All of this happened so suddenly and here I am fifty-four years of age. I do not want history to be repeated for you."

I told him I was glad he was okay and not to talk of such things. Deep down inside I silently agreed with him. I was only 16 at the time, the same age as my father when he first saw the Statue of Liberty.

The second event was devastating not only to me but greatly affected my dad. My cousin, Marty, who had been working in the barbershop for Dad for two years, contracted Hodgkin's Lymphoma, a rare form of lymphatic cancer that attacks the lymph nodes. In 1965 there was no known cure for this fatal disease, although some survived with special medication for a few years. In spite of all the attempts to save him, Marty died in December 1966.

Naturally, everyone in the family was distraught for no family member had died since patriarch Vincenzo in 1934. I was distraught to have lost someone who was like a brother to me. We shared many moments in the daily grind of the barbershop. Marty and I were close in age and I helped him around the barber chair as I continued to learn about the trade. During his apprenticeship he invited me to spend a few days with him at barber school. I thought it would be fun so we took the evening train and departed for Cleveland.

Marty, always up to something, started as soon as the train pulled out of the station.

"Perry, do you know how you can tell which women on this train are Italian?"

"No, Marty, but I know you're going to tell me."

As he started to grab his mid-section in preparation for a full belly laugh, Marty answered, "They are the ones with the moustaches!"

He had a great sense of humor and we spent our time on the train ride to Cleveland laughing so hard we frequently came to tears. Most of our humor was centered on our Italian heritage and the unique way of life that only descendants of immigrants can relate to with regards to their old-fashioned ways.

I remember during Marty's early diagnosis that he was hospitalized and heavily medicated. I stopped by to see him on the way to one of my senior year high school football games. He quietly told me as I departed, "I'll listen to the game on the radio tonight. I'm sorry I can't be there to watch you guys play." Here he was lying in agony and he tells *me* that he was sorry he couldn't be at the stadium as he rarely missed one of my games. I scored my share of touchdowns that evening as we handily won the football game. When I saw him the next day, he sleepily told me, "Hey, every time I woke up during the game it seemed like you were scoring a touchdown. Who was playing on the opposing team, a bunch of girls?"

I recall coming apart at his funeral at the thought of not having Marty around anymore to listen or watch me score touchdowns. It was quite selfish of me for, as I scanned my surroundings, I noticed that my aunt and uncle were not doing very well with the loss of their son at the age of twenty-three. Raffaela was very upset at the loss of a grandchild and as I reached over to console her I noticed my father, the consummate family man, had his arm around her, doing his best to contain the utter sadness that was overwhelming him.

"Mamma, don't despair. Just keep thinking of how Papa will surely greet young Marty in Heaven."

Sure, he lost one of his well-liked young barbers but more poignantly he lost part of his bloodline.

The atmosphere in Dad's shop changed in more ways than could have been predicted after Marty's death and the loss of one of his barbers. The business was booming as the 1960s came to a close but the culture in this country produced a dramatic change in not only how we acted but also how we looked. Long hair became a fad. Gone were the days of men between the ages of thirteen and forty getting their hair cut every couple of

My Father's Compass

weeks. In fact, some would go three to four months without a haircut, and because it was so long, they started showing up at the local beauty parlors. If a barbershop got onboard with this fad, special hairstyling techniques became the primary way to avoid losing clientele. Dad, however, tried his best to continue and maintain the traditional barbershop venue. He really thought that this craze would pass.

"I'm not going to get involved with this nonsense," he would often say.

"Men and boys will get over this soon and change their minds about having long hair."

Stubborn and very determined, he was forced to shut down one chair at a time and in the mid-1970s closed down the front of his barbershop and moved to the back room as a two-chair shop. He was about to curtail his once flourishing barber business where he had started. Unfortunately, he had a hard time finding someone to fill the second chair and he resorted to some retired barber friends to come in on Saturdays and help him cut the hair of young boys brought in by mothers not willing to let their hair grow too long.

In 1976, Dad and Mom were settling into their later life as empty nesters and they sold their post World War II house and moved a few blocks away to a smaller and more comfortable home. Mother Raffaela reluctantly slept for the last time in her attached apartment built in 1954 by the hands of her sons.

Finally, in 1987 at the age of seventy-seven, Dad completely closed the barbershop, sixty years after his arrival at Ellis Island. He had walked to work since they moved or drove the few blocks to the shop during inclement weather. His customer base was actually dying off. He found himself spending many evenings at local funeral homes, cutting former customers' hair as a final gift before they were laid to rest. He did this willingly and with a sense of loyalty and service to those who had been so good to him over the years.

He had been a mainstay as a local barber in this Northeastern Ohio town for over fifty years and, when he walked away from his chair, he never looked back except to reflect on the great memories of a great career and a wonderful legacy.

Dad passed away gently in his sleep of a failing heart on December 16, 1994. He was eighty-four.

When a son of such a man looks back on his own life, it is inspirational to reflect on the many lessons one has learned. Dad taught me many facets about life from the lessons he passed on. I have realized over the years that I am much like him. I learned from him as he learned from his own father and all those people in his life he emulated—observe and learn. Dad was always one who let me know exactly where I stood and, growing up under his tutelage, did not completely appreciate the extent of his leadership style or how his fundamental approach seemed to always work. He literally taught himself everything he needed to know following his arrival to America in 1927.

There is no doubt as to his naïve immigrant status as a sixteen-year-old stepping off the boat at Ellis Island. He had attended only two years of grammar school in Italy and would have been illiterate were it not for the fact he taught himself how to read and write while traversing the hills of Italy as a shepherd and cheese maker. His first and immediate goal was to immerse himself in learning the English language so he could fully assimilate into society and become a serving citizen of the American landscape. In three short years, he could read and write in both English and Italian and was very adept in the use of the standard ink pen that produced beautiful calligraphy when he wrote. And write he did.

Right up until his last days of life, he remained the conduit between family members in the United States and those who remained in Italy and would rarely skip a month or two without writing a long letter to his cousins in Rivisondoli. He was revered in those hills as a hero and the family that remained spoke of him as if he was an Italian-American literary laureate.

I had the special privilege of being with my dad when he made what turned out to be his only return to his hometown village of Rivisondoli. It was a special moment for my dad and me. He took me to his first home and showed me his place of birth. As we stood at the front door of this little shack called a house, tears welled in his eyes as he recalled the departure in March 1927.

"We had no idea what was to come," Dad said, struggling to speak through the emotional experience. "I grabbed Mario's hand right there as we walked down the hill and don't think I ever let him out of my sight until we got on the train in New York heading for Ohio. I used to sit right here in front of this small house and look onto the valley and dream of the future. Look at us now. I own a barbershop in America and you are about to become a Naval Officer. Phew. Give me a hug, son."

I happily obliged and fought back my own tears of reflection that I shared with my father as we proudly stood together on those hills of Rivisondoli, Italy, and looked down on the valley. We took a little walk down the hill and re-created his 1927 departure.

Instinctively, Dad reached over and held my hand.

Whenever I make the trip back to *my* hometown, I make it a habit to pass the Martinis' first home back in Warren, Ohio. I purposely slow the car down to take it all in and I try to see the house through my dad's young eyes that eventful day in 1927. I try to comprehend the emotional experience that overcomes me to connect the old to the new and, when reflecting on the crash of the stock market on Black Monday in America in 1929, it's difficult to have an appreciation for just how unfair it must have seemed to those huddled in their new environment on First Street in their new humble abode.

There's much to be learned about how my father helped raise his family after his dad passed away during the Great Depression. I firmly believe that when one speaks of Italian-American values, they speak mostly about faith and family; everything else is a distant third. My father loved his brothers and sister very much for they had been through hell together from the rough voyage on the *Cristoforo Columbo* to making ends meet while surviving abject poverty. He spoke often of wishing he could have traded places with his dad and be the one the good Lord took home; he made the same comment when young Marty, Jr. died.

On his deathbed, he was more focused on his wife, Angie, than his own demise. When it came to family, there was nothing Dad wouldn't do to help or support a family member in need. His servant leadership, strong and abiding faith, and family values were forged over a lifetime in how he treated and loved others as if they were all family. Perhaps that is the simplest description of servant leadership when discussing family in the same breath—Dad loved his family unconditionally.

It is important that I not neglect the irony of my dad and his love for his youngest brother, Mario. I often think of them huddled together during the crossing and how it came to be that both cemented their relationship while at sea on a voyage over the great Atlantic. It is no small coincidence that they both entered the United States Navy during World War II. Mario took full advantage of his opportunity to receive an education and used his sheer determination to become a blimp pilot as a Naval Officer. Dad used his talents as a servant leader and became a leading Petty Officer in a barbershop on the *USS Rocky Mount.*

No one was prouder of Mario than Dad, and no one was prouder of Dad than Mario while they both served their *new* country by returning to the mighty oceans to fight for freedom. The connection goes even deeper, for as I observed my dad over the years and listened to his sea stories of decks, bulkheads, and shipboard life, I also took notice and a keen interest in the fact that my uncle Mario had become a career Naval Officer. It was my first fascination with forming my own vision that I wanted very badly to join the Navy like my father had done and to become a Navy pilot like my uncle.

I got my wish on June 28, 1967, when I raised my hand and took an oath of office to become a midshipman at the United States Naval Academy in Annapolis, Maryland.

Three days later, my uncle Mario retired as a Captain, United States Navy.

It is hard to put into words the exhilaration on my dad's face when our eyes met at the end of my plebe summer training in Annapolis. I was in my sparkling white Navy uniform and I had proudly survived the first hurdle. He and Mom had returned to Annapolis for parents' weekend and at first we couldn't find each other. Remember, this was 1967 and there were no cell phones. Oddly, when I saw him walking from a distance, I recognized him by his distinct gait. The first thought that popped into my mind was the story of my dad frantically searching and finally seeing his father at Ellis Island. I was feeling the same rush come over me for my dad's proud smile spoke volumes of how he felt as well. I also realized that it had been only three months for us to be apart and that it was unimaginable to be separated by an ocean from a father for nearly six years.

"Mom, Dad, this place is really something. Actually, the summer has gone by quickly, but I must tell you that I am most impressed with what they are teaching us regarding core values—courage, honor, and commitment."

Dad only smiled. I knew that he was speechless, which I now look back on as a rare moment in time, but he fully realized that this set of values was no different from the value system he brought with him from Italy and passed on to me by his example as a servant leader.

Dad was always someone who could be counted on no matter what the task. He never learned to say no to those who were in need of his assistance. When Dad made a commitment, he was true to his word. His acts of service were legendary and, although there might have been a few people who took advantage of his good nature, he never let that bother him, and instead was joyful about the opportunity to help. To be honorable was indeed important and, as I clearly remember in my younger days, it was at the top of the Italian-American value system.

I learned an important lesson on why being honorable was critically important. On one such occasion I experienced a stern scolding by my dad brought on by my own volition. I frequently was asked to run down the street late in the afternoon to purchase a fresh loaf of homemade Italian bread at a local bakery. Dad pulled a quarter out of the barbershop cash register one day and asked to me hurry for the bakery was closing in five minutes. Three days later he asked me what I did with the change from the quarter since he knew the loaf of bread cost only twenty cents.

My answer was typical of a young boy caught in a web of deceit for I responded, "What change?"

"How dare you question me? Don't you know by now that I am not stupid? The bread costs twenty cents. Where is the change?"

I was instructed to retrieve the nickel I had obviously kept for myself, and as I walked into the basement tunnel it hit me that I had hid more than just one nickel in my secret hiding space. When I stooped down to retrieve the nickel behind a basement counter leg, I wisely grabbed the other handful of nickels that I was stashing. As I turned around, I was in the presence of my father who had followed me to my hidden basement bank.

"Give me all of it!"

Taking the coins from my hand, he sternly said, "Never, ever steal from me again for you are taking food off the table!"

"I want you to think long and hard about what you have done. I want you to be a man of honor and character. Don't be petty about wanting things in life. 'Dogommit,' no one in our family has ever gone to jail and you better not be the first!"

I knew he was angry and although I never heard him swear or use profanity, he often used words he made up to avoid taking God's name in vain when he was truly upset. In this instance he did not punish or spank me although he had every right to discipline me. He just asked me to never do it again and to give him my word.

"Yes, Papa. I am truly sorry and it won't happen again." I had a large pit in my stomach and never forgot this incident.

Later, when I was a little older, Dad asked me to man the cash register on Saturdays so his barbers didn't have to worry about taking time out of the very busy schedule to also cash out the customers. Dad and I had gone full circle as he trusted me and knew inherently I wouldn't help myself to loose change. He knew I had learned my lesson about not stealing. During my four years at the Naval Academy, the honor concept was not foreign to my moral compass for I had indeed never forgotten the simple lessons of never lying, cheating, or stealing.

While I worked hard at the Naval Academy, I also mismanaged my time with reckless abandon. Playing sports and being involved in a multitude of extracurricular activities led me to be on the border of flunking out at the end of so many semesters that I hesitate to mention the number. Dad knew I was struggling and he told me to not worry and that I could always come home to help him with the barber business. It reminded me of our little talk when I was a junior in high school.

"Perry, you have two choices regarding attending college," Dad said when we were talking about my future. "You either get a scholarship, or you go to barber school."

In other words, there is no savings or college fund and you will have to get there on your own or join me in the business. I knew deep down inside Dad would have been thrilled if I had chosen to follow in his footsteps. But, as he recognized in his youngest brother, Mario, nearly three decades earlier, he knew that I had the potential to be something besides a barber. It truly never bothered him for it was part of his vision of life that his children would be beneficiaries of the prosperity America had to offer. My flunking out of the Naval Academy would have devastated him. He bragged incessantly behind the barber chair about his son at Annapolis who was going to be a Navy pilot. I was never quite sure if I was motivated solely for my own sake to graduate from Annapolis or more concerned about hurting my father.

Nevertheless, there was no one prouder than Dad on June 9, 1971, when he watched me throw my midshipmen hat into the air at the graduation and commissioning ceremony. He hugged me tightly moments later and had tears streaming down his cheeks with pride.

"Perry, well done. You make me so happy and proud."

To this day, I can visualize that emotional moment. There he stood—the Italian immigrant who clawed his way to the shores of America, struggled mightily as the surrogate father for his family during the Depression, fought bravely as a member of the Greatest Generation during World War II, and who successfully raised a family. There he stood with tears of joy that his son made it and would now be in the same U.S. Navy he had come to love. My military journey and career started that day and, as I reflect back on my dad's humble start with that one chair on his front porch back in 1948, my start was no different in that challenges and opportunities awaited me. Dad had finished completing part of his vision and now the lessons passed down to me were about to be placed in motion.

Dad wrote often during my Navy career for I was constantly globetrotting and his letters would catch up with me sooner or later. His letters were a welcome sight for I missed talking to him. At times I would receive his letters right before I jumped in my aircraft to fly a mission somewhere thousands of miles from home. I would save the letter for when I was not in the cockpit and read it back in the galley of my Navy P-3 Orion. He never wrote a short letter. His double-sided letters were prolific and he always wrote the postscript on the backside of the final page by using the side margin of the parchment paper. He spoke often about our family and would always pass Mom and Grandma's love to me. Mom would send cards and add a short note, while Raffaela would place an "X" somewhere near the bottom followed by a few "Os." I knew what she meant and that's all that counted. Dad admired his mother and although he understood his dad's vision, he hardly got to know him like he knew his mom. She was a true believer and her love of faith and family was legendary. I learned a lifelong lesson from her regarding parents and children during one of my brief visits while on leave.

Little did I know that it was to be one of the last private visits with my *nonna* when I spent some time with grandma Raffaela in her apartment kitchen at the end of one of my infrequent visits to my hometown in 1975. We chatted about the old country, her long life (she was ninety-three at the time), and, of course, the family. She started to cry and I asked her what was wrong. Through the tears she told me in her dialect Italian, "My children!" I struggled to find the words and quizzed her as to why she would be worried about her children since they were all by this time in their 70s and were grandparents themselves. She quickly responded, "They are still *my* children and don't ever forget it!" Of course! Why should I be perplexed? *La famiglia e sempre importante*—The family is always of the utmost importance.

Over the years, I was never quite sure why but I filled empty shoeboxes with all of my dad's letters and kept them in a safe place. Many were written while I was flying overseas in some far away corner of the world. One such letter, however, holds a special place in my "shoebox" of memories. It was written and sent shortly after I assumed command of Patrol Squadron 10 in Brunswick, Maine.

10-16-1987

Caro Perry,

It seems only yesterday since we left you but 3 weeks have gone by very fast. Sorry for not writing sooner to express how immensely emotional we enjoyed dearly and the happy few days together twenty days ago when you took command of the Squadron. It was a great day for you and we are indeed so proud of what you have accomplished. It was a grand and glorious day, for here in front of my very eyes I was watching my son become the Capitano of his command. My words cannot describe what a momentious [sic] occasion this was indeed. I was so glad that your mother was able to travel and able to sit next to me and take it all in. We both cried together as we were honored by your words of gratitude to us for raising you well. The marvelous accommodations you provided for us at the hotel and yes, the special driver and car that picked us up for all the events. Heck— we were really special people and you made sure we knew it! Jean's parents too. They enjoyed all the special treatment and mother and I enjoyed immensely getting to know them better. Of course, seeing my young brother, Mario, arrive at the hotel the night before the big event was quite the surprise. You must know deep down inside how good this made me feel. Here was my brother, a retired Navy Captain, showing up for my son's change of the command. Neither one of us could have ever imagined such a day when we were huddled together on the Cristoforo Colombo and crossing the Atlantic in 1927. Perry, this was the first time I ever had the opportunity to hear you speak in front of people. As you splendidly addressed the group assembled, especially those young men and women you are taking command of, I couldn't help but think of how great a job you will do in caring for each and every one of them. As I listened intently, I knew deep in my heart that you will take care of them just like my senior officers took care of me when I was on the USS Rocky Mount during WWII. My heart was filled with pride and joy when you honored your dear father by your elequent [sic] words about how you learned so much from me on how to be a good leader. Perry, I never realized the impact I must have made. I didn't know and I really am happy you shared this with so many to hear. I have to stop for a few minuti for I must wipe my eyes. I know there is much ahead for you as you continue your naval career. Mother will *continue to worry about your flying. She can't pray enough for your safety. I know you will always do your best and become a great leader in the U.S. Navy. Be proud for where you have come from and never forget the vision of your grandfather, Vincenzo. Without his persistence we would not have been able to enjoy watching you take command and be a proud American! Perry, you know it's been now sixty years since we have made our way to this great land. You have made a dream come true for all of us in the family...Mother and I are proud of you and we can go to our rest someday knowing that our effort to becoming Americans was all the worthwhile. All my love, respect and admiration for you and best of fortune and blessings, Skipper!*

As always your mom and dad,
Perry and Angie

P.S. Perry, hard to believe I am 77 years young today! I made a decision this morning that I intend to fully retire and shut down the Barber Shop. It's been a great career.

During my time in command, Dad and I had numerous conversations about my daily activities at the squadron. He was always most interested in how "my people" were doing. He was never concerned about the myriad of issues and decisions I had to make but he was most interested in how I was treating those who worked for me. His insights on what leadership was had more meaning to me as I matured as a senior officer in the Navy. He knew that "my people" couldn't care less about what or how much I knew, but simply knew that I cared.

Dad's legacy was the impact he had on those who knew him and for me they were enduring lessons of life. He made certain that we never forgot our roots. All of us who were descendants of the family bloodline had been the beneficiaries of the vision established by my father that was a continuation of the dream passed on by his father, Vincenzo. Faith, family, friends, and country were at the center of these lessons. Many of us who now are far removed from this mass immigration of the 20th century have so much to be grateful for as proud citizens of this great country. I sometimes pretend to be perched on the *Cristoforo Colombo* much like my dad and make a feeble attempt to re-create the crossing in my mind. The lesson learned is an obvious one: liberty is worth the fight and freedom is worth the struggle to attain. Live your dreams and have hope in your heart.

One of the lasting lessons that my father left as a legacy was his love, loyalty, and devotion to *my* mother. He never wavered from his commitment to her and kept her in the highest place of his regard and admiration. He worried constantly in his latter years for he was fearful that he would not be able to take care of Mom when they both grew old. Mom had an unfortunate accident when she was sixty and broke her hip. She never walked without a cane or walker for the remainder of her life. Dad doted on her and was the ever-consummate caretaker. Seven years her senior, he did everything he could to live as long as possible so as to not leave her a grieving widow.

When Dad was becoming a danger driving his car a year before he died, I had the misfortune to be the bearer of bad news for him by taking away the car keys. It took me an entire weekend to conjure up the nerve to take his car keys away from him. It was an emotional event and I do not like to reflect on it. I do recall that the one issue that caused him to give me his keys was the fear I placed on him that, if something happened to him while driving, Mom would be left without a husband.

"Dad, you know I've been meaning to talk to you about the car and your driving since I arrived home for the weekend. Before I leave we need to discuss this situation."

Struggling to not show his despair, Dad quickly said, "Please, Perry, don't do this to me. The car and my driving and running errands keep me independent and I promise to be careful."

"Dad, you have had too many close calls lately. What would happen if you hit someone or worse yet run over a little boy or girl on a bicycle? Your entire insurance policy would be wiped out and you could be put in jail. What will happen to Mom then? Have you ever thought about this?"

I really was stretching the truth here but I had to embellish what could occur in the hopes of his seeing through this without a struggle or argument. He settled down for a moment and gave this some serious thought.

"Perry, if you must, and this is for the best for Mom, then it will be all right."

He didn't like thinking about what effect his poor driving could have on Mom and, after many tears and his begging me not to take the car, I did what I knew was right—I took the car away from him.

I chose to end this book in articulating these enduring lessons I learned from my father's compass. Much of the lessons that were passed on to me made me a better leader and paved the way to my becoming a Navy Captain. I replicated my uncle Mario's career path and fulfilled my boyhood dream of flying as a Naval Aviator, but I had plenty of help along the way. I am proud of being a first generation Italian-American. My father's legacy was that we would never forget our humble beginnings and to be thankful for what we have become. He consistently made it his trademark to be of service to others and to always find a way to contribute to society and therefore make a difference.

It is a call to service as a free American I have never forgotten.

Moreover, there is little doubt that I was forever linked to my father's compass at each and every turn in the road to success as a leader. Dad's lessons in life were simple and filled with love. He was selfless and the kind of man one wants to emulate. His story is not unique as an immigrant.

It is a story we descendants must never forget and bears repeating for generations to come.

Epilogue

I wrote this book about my father and about the vision he inherited from his father and how their determination and perseverance impacted my personal and professional life. My story as a direct descendant of immigrants is not unique since today nearly thirty million, or one in every ten, Americans have some Italian blood and a link with someone who shared this vision of coming to *"la Medica."* My grandfather started thinking about this journey as a young man in the hills of Italy in 1898. Today, well over one hundred years later, Italian-Americans comprise the fifth largest ethnic group in the United States according to the U.S. Census Bureau. The four larger groups are: Germans, Irish, English, and African-Americans.

As I reflect on the events of the 20th century, I come to the biased conclusion that immigrants who came from Italy made quite a significant impact on our society. It would be so exhilarating to be able to sit down with Vincenzo Martini and tell him about the direct descendants who became household names in *"la Medica."* The partial list of names reads like an Italian-American Hall of Fame in nearly every walk of life: Cuomo, Guiliano, Grasso, Rodino, LaGuardia, Paca, Celebrezze, Ferraro, Sirica, Scalia, and Alito (Government); DeNiro, Sinatra, Como, Lombardo, Lanza, Bono, Coppola, Durante, Capra,

Stallone, Valentino, and Funicello (Entertainment); Lasorda, Andretti, Mosconi, Dimaggio, Berra, Marciano, Basilio, Arcaro, Torre, Campanella, Paterno, Lombardi, Bellino, Montana, and Marino (Sports); Iaccoca, Giannini, Gharadelli, Jacuzzi, Cafaro, DeBartolo, Riggio, Gallo, and Rossi (Business and Industry); Cabrini, Grasso, Giamatti, Pellegrino, and Sammartino (Education). The only enlisted Marine in U.S. history to win the nation's highest military honors, the Navy Cross and the Medal of Honor, was John Basilone, a descendant of immigrant parents, who died at the Battle of Iwo Jima during World War II. Today, Marine General Peter Pace, another Italian-American, is the Chairman of the Joint Chiefs of Staff, the most senior military post in the U.S. Armed Forces. Another Marine General and first generation Italian-American, Anthony Zinni, commanded the U.S. Central Command during Operations Iraqi and Enduring Freedom. My dad's contribution was a microcosm to the universe of culture that now permeates our American way of life. Similar to many of his native countrymen, Dad lived his life to the fullest as he was convicted by faith that the course he steered was indeed guided by a power energized by the strength of his spiritual faith.

When I retired from the United States Navy in 1998, I had the opportunity to give a farewell address in Memorial Hall at the United States Naval Academy. I was positioned in this grand room at the podium facing the entrance door that opened below on to Tecumseh Court. It was in that very court thirty-one years before that I stood taking an oath of service to our country and to the U.S. Navy. I couldn't help think of my father, who intently watched that ceremony nearby and the joy and pride in his eyes that was apparent after we bid each other adieu in 1967. I spoke now, many years later, of how much I missed my dad but recalled how he set the course for being a success in life. It was a simple lesson he passed along that if you want to excel then it would be wise to follow the example of others and to "observe and learn." It was really how he was able to be a success in life for he would emulate those he admired, starting with his father and ending quite ironically with his son.

As I reflect on who I have become, I realize that I spent much of my early life choosing my own attitude, often with self in mind and for no better reason than to indulge self-satisfaction. My grandfather and father were selfless human beings who always placed their faith in God and their love for others before their own self-interests. They are my heroes, and as I write of their service to the noble causes of World War I and World War II, I gain a greater appreciation and respect for why they served. They were not men of spotless virtue, but they were honest, brave, and loyal all of their lives.

I learned immensely from these men, enduring lessons of life that only determined people could pass down to their heirs. I learned to persevere and to always know that it was worth trying to be the best I could possibly be in spite of any obstacles. I consider myself extraordinarily fortunate to be the beneficiary of their great vision. Following my father's compass and having the good sense to remember only the good in him helps me follow the course he set for me all the more. His name will never appear on the Italian-American list of the famous, but he will be remembered among many as a man who served his God, his family, his country, and his friends well. It is fitting that the following biblical quote from Matthew is prominent on his tombstone: "Well done, good and faithful servant."

I feel a special kinship with the descendants of those who immigrated to this wonderful land of opportunity. We all have inherited unique characteristics and ethnicity that is recognizable and distinguishable as to our roots. Less obvious are the intangibles that can in certain lives make all the difference. One cannot define, for example, family values, but it is evident to the casual observer when they are among those who cherish this treasure. Those who witnessed first hand the greeting by the Great Lady who stands proudly in New York Harbor had no earthly idea how their vision would play out, but they were determined to do their best in reaching that dream.

General Pete Pace, Chairman of the Joint Chiefs of Staff, recently spoke eloquently of his Italian heritage and said, "There is no country on the planet that affords the kind of opportunity to those who come here. I am proud to be a descendant of a generation of Italian men and women who made their way to this country in the 20th century. We live free and prosperous today by fulfilling their vision of a great opportunity to become freedom-loving people."

God bless America, land that I love.

Acknowledgments

A book that reflects one's roots is difficult to complete without the help of those who are closest to you, which, of course, includes one's family. I am grateful to my wife, Jean, and daughter, Elle, for taking the time to personally edit my work. Without their help, my message would not have the clarity regarding not only my heritage but that of servant leadership. I also thank my Italian-born friend, Dominic Petruzzi, for checking my Italian while proofreading my final manuscripts.

A special thanks to my cousins who assisted me in locating the photos that I have shared with you in the center of this book. Thanks to Ginny Martini Lucarelli, Phyllis Martini Golloway, Laura Martini Jansen, Jerry Martini, and my sister, Marie Martini Balista, for providing the photos and for sharing their reflections of our dads over the years. Phyllis's son, John, appears on the front cover in my dad's barber chair and could pass for any one of us who resemble the Martini Italian heritage. Every male in my extended family appeared in my dad's chair at one time or another during their lifetime, and two of them stood next to him in later years as fellow barbers. All of my cousins are like brothers and sisters to each other and we are connected, as Vincenzo himself would have wanted as part of a fulfillment of his dream. Only a few of us ever got to meet him before he died tragically in 1934, and those few were very young. Only four of the twenty-four of us have passed away and as you read in this book, Marty (Eraldo, Jr.) was the first to go at the young age of twenty-two in 1966. Since then, Vince and Ron (Joe's sons) have passed away and have been recently followed by Almerinda's son, Galvin DePompei.

As I listened to those who eulogized my cousin Galvin at his funeral in March 2006, I was struck by the message that was indeed so clear about how he lived his life. He was truly remembered as a servant leader, one who gave completely of himself to his family, community, and country. He was a shining example of that fulfilled vision of a grandfather he never got to meet or know, Vincenzo, but truly followed his compass. He, like all of us, had the faith that we will be reunited with our parents and grandparents in eternity and will be able to thank them for the life and opportunity they truly gave us on earth.

References

Bennett, William J. *Why We Fight*, Regnery, 2002.

Bradley, James. *Flags of Our Fathers*, Bantam, 2000.

Fisher, R. Stewart and Martini, Perry J. *Inspiring Leadership: Character and Ethics Matter*, Academy Leadership Publishing, 2004.

Greenleaf, Robert K. *The Servant as a Leader*, The Greenleaf Center, 1991.

Hemingway, Ernest. *A Farewell to Arms*, Charles Scribner's Sons, 1929.

McCain, John. *Faith of My Fathers*, Random House, 1999.

Ruggero, Ed and Haley, Dennis F. *The Leader's Compass, 2nd Edition: A Personal Leadership Philosophy Is Your Key to Success*, Academy Leadership Publishing, 2005.

Ruggero, Ed and Haley, Dennis F. *The Corporate Compass: Providing Focus and Alignment to Stay the Course*, Academy Leadership Publishing, 2005.

BOOKS FROM ACADEMY LEADERSHIP PUBLISHING

My Father's Compass: Leadership Lessons for an Immigrant Son
(2006, ISBN: 0-9727323-4-9, $17.95)
by Perry J. Martini

The Leader's Compass: A Personal Leadership Philosophy Is Your Key to Success, 2nd Edition
(2005, ISBN: 0-9727323-1-4, $17.95)
by Ed Ruggero and Dennis F. Haley

The Corporate Compass: Providing Focus and Alignment to Stay the Course
(2005, ISBN: 0-9727323-3-0, $17.95)
by Ed Ruggero and Dennis F. Haley

Inspiring Leadership: Character and Ethics Matter
(2005, ISBN: 0-9727323-2-2, $24.95)
by R. Stewart Fisher and Perry J. Martini

Academy Leadership books are available at special quantity discounts to use as premiums and sales promotions, or for use in corporate training programs. For more information, please call Academy Leadership at 866-783-0630, visit www.academyleadership.com, or write to: 10120 Valley Forge Circle, King of Prussia, PA 19406.